To: Gundy

From: Terry

Christmas 1986.

MONASTERIES OF NORFOLK

by the same author

A COMPLETE DESCRIPTIVE GUIDE TO BRITISH MONUMENTAL
BRASSES Thames & Hudson 1972

Richard Le Strange

MONASTERIES
OF NORFOLK

YATES PUBLISHING

© Richard Le Strange 1973

Published in 1973 by Yates Publications, 1 St James' Street, King's Lynn, Norfolk

Printed by Daedalus Press, Stoke Ferry, King's Lynn, Norfolk

ACKNOWLEDGEMENTS

Many thanks are due to the Rev C J W Messent
for permission to use his book entitled *The Monastic
Remains of Norfolk and Suffolk,* published by himself
in June 1934; and to the Norfolk and Norwich
Archælogical Society, for the use of their library.

Monastic Norfolk until the Dissolution

TYPES OF ESTABLISHMENTS TO BE FOUND IN NORFOLK:

Monks: Benedictine, Cluniac, Cistercian.
Canons Regular: Augustinian, Premonstratension.
Double Houses: Gilbertine Nuns and Canons.
Nuns and Canonesses: Benedictine, Cistercian, Augustinian.
Trinitarian: Order of the Holy Trinity and St Victor for the Redemption of Captives.
Friars: Austin, Carmelite, Dominican, Franciscan, Of the Sack of Lesser Orders.
Knights Templars.
Knights Hospitallers.
Hospitals.
Monastic Granges or Manors.

THE BENEDICTINE MONKS

Benedictine monks take their name from St Benedict of Nursia. He created the Rule which they follow and was born at Nursia or Norcia, near Spoleto in Central Italy, about the year 480, of rich parents.

He studied in Rome and withdrew to live in a cave at Subiaco, some thirty miles from the city.

His fame soon spread and before long he had numerous followers. These he organised into several communities. He then moved southward to found at Monte Cassino the most famous monastery of his Order. It was built on the site of a heathen temple about 525. Here St Benedict lived until his death *c.* 550.

The first Benedictine monks to come to England landed in Thanet in 597. Pope Gregory the Great (590 - 604) sent them. When he was an Abbot in Rome he had seen English slaves sold on the slave market there. He was touched by their plight and later sent missionaries to convert England. He chose the Kingdom of Kent as a base because the king there had married a Christian princess from France who would help and back them.

Several monasteries were founded and things looked well for the Order. Then the unexpected happened. In 793, the Vikings landed at the Island of Lindisfarne, sacked the monastery and killed some of the monks. The people were horrified. They thought it impossible that the Viking pirates could make such a journey, but they had.

With their shallow draft boats they could manage almost any stream or river, which they did, to terrorise, plunder and kill. Naturally monasteries were obvious centres of attack, being completely defenceless and owning valuable plate and treasure for the taking.

Within one hundred years of the attack on Lindisfarne, the structure of English monastic life had almost completely perished. From time to time attempts were made to restore the damage, but these did not meet with much success until the mid-tenth century.

The process of revival began in 943 with the restoration of conventual discipline at Glastonbury. From then monastic life began anew and did not look back.

The Battle of Hastings in 1066, led to William Duke of Normandy being crowned King of England. For almost fifty years the foundation of monasteries was fairly slow, but by 1100, about one hundred new Benedictine houses had been founded, although some were 'alien priories' or cells or dependant houses given to foreign monasteries by the barons of the Norman Conquest. Some of these cells were very small and served very little use.

St Benedict himself was a hermit. He conceived the idea of bringing together a group of such men and uniting them under a definite Rule over which he presided. Each community of monks was an independent body living under its own Abbot. They owed no allegiance to any central body.

Their day was divided up into a regular series of services, contemplations, study and the work of the convent. The first service was at 2 a.m. Matins, followed by Lauds at 4.30 a.m., 6 a.m. Prime, 9 a.m. Terse, Sext at noon, 3 p.m. Nones, 4.30 p.m. Vespers, and Compline at 6 p.m. After a while Matins and Lauds were taken together at midnight. Later there was a tendency to join other services. On Sunday, Mass was sung during the forenoon, but later it was sung daily.

As the Order grew in numbers and influence, it became the custom to employ servants to carry out manual work, this enabled the monks to continue the more important tasks such as the writing of books, carrying out Divine service and tending the sick.

As with most human institutions, abuses and slackness crept in and various reforms were effected from time to time.

The Benedictine or Black monks as they were called were usually found in towns. Their principal houses were Abbeys and their cells called priories.

CLUNIAC ORDER OF MONKS

The Cluniac Order was founded in England by William de Warenne, first Earl of Surrey. He came to England with William the Conquereor and died in the year 1088.

The Earl and his wife Gundrada, visited the famous Abbey of Cluny in Burgundy and had been admitted into the fraternity of the Order. This visit was some time before 1077. The

[9]

Earl was very moved by the sight of this splendid monastery and its ordered life and endless round of devotion.

When he came to England he brought with him the desire to found a religious house. As a result the Priory of St Pancras at Lewes was established and three monks of Cluny with their Prior Lanzo, were settled near the castle of their founder.

The first Cluniac house in Norfolk was at Castleacre, being an offshoot of the Priory of Lewes. This is thought to have been founded *c*. 1090.

The Priory at Lewes had the precedence over the other houses of the English province, but it was a precedence of honour rather than authority.

The Cluniac monks were a reformed order of Benedictines, carrying out a stricter interpretation of the Benedictine rules, but, like all monastic institutions, after a time as wealth increased, abuses became apparent and in time its place as a reformed Order was taken by the Cistercians.

Originally the mother house at Cluny in Burgundy was a Benedictine Abbey founded by the Duke of Aquitaine in 940. It was subject directly to the Pope and with the aid of various papal privileges gradually became head of a separate order. This order became very powerful and wealthy with very ornate buildings and services.

Their houses were also called priories. They owed allegiance to the Abbey of Cluny in Burgundy.

THE CISTERCIANS OR WHITE MONKS

The mother house of the Cistercian Order was Citeaux, not far from Dijon in northern Burgundy.

A party of monks under one called Robert, in 1098, left their mother house of Molesme to found a stricter one. They were convinced that the life at Molesme was too easy going. Their life in their new house was a very hard one at first, but fairly quickly the situation changed due to the wise abbacy of an Englishman, Stephen Harding, who ruled Citeaux from

1109 to 1134. With the help of St Bernard, Abbot of the daughter house of Clairvaux, the new order made great strides.

The monks lived in a community like Benedictines or Cluniacs but were rather Puritanical in their outlook. Their buildings were plain, with no ornamentations of any kind. There were no sculptures, silk vestments, no gold or silver vessels, only pewter.

They avoided towns and built their abbeys in remote places. Because of this they were unable to obtain servants so they had a special group of men in each abbey to do the manual work. This was done by lay brothers or conversi, who took monastic vows but were illiterate.

These lay brothers lived in the west range and performed all the menial tasks of the abbey. It was the Cistercians who first developed sheep farming in England.

The first house in England was founded at Waverley in 1128. All the houses had to have at least thirteen brethren and no two were to be found close together.

In Norfolk there was no Abbey for the Cistercian monks, at Pentney, however, there was a priory for Cistercian nuns.

The Cistercian monasteries were always called Abbeys and the nunneries were always called Priories.

THE CANONS
SECULARS

For the first 1000 A.D. years, the clergy were secular, that is they lived in the world and worked with ordinary people. There were a few exceptions, being the priests who became monks.

A canon was originally a priest on the official list of diocesan clergy, as distinct from one serving in a monastery. In the Dark Ages most of such official clergy lived in large clergy houses or collegiate churches. Canon became the name of one of these living in such an institution as distinct from one living on his own.

They should have been unmarried, but they were under no obligation to take any vow of poverty. Before the Norman Conquest, official rule for such canons was that they should have a common refectory and dormitory and also draw their stipends from a common fund.

In the mid-eleventh century there was a movement on the Continent to make life in these minsters, or collegiate churches, more severe. This movement won the support of the chief reformers of the day including the future Pope Gregory VII. The matter was given official consideration at the Lateran synod of 1059 and a reasonable compromise was reached.

The council commended the idea of clergy living in effect the monastic life, that is, being unmarried, living without property, being obedient to a common superior. However, the council did not force such a decision on the clergy of the day. The canons of the old way of life became known as 'secular canons,' because they lived in the world (seculum) and not in a strict community.

The canons who wished to follow the newer code had it officially approved in 1059 and were known as 'regular canons,' that is, canons living by a Regular or Rule.

AUGUSTINIAN CANONS

The idea of a common life based on that of monks appealed to a great many clergy. Gradually the regular canons adopted the so called Rule of St Augustine of Hippo, from which they derived the name, Augustinian.

They worked in the parishes around their priories, but in the priory itself, lived much the same as a monk would. They had a common dormitory, refectory, chapter house and infirmary.

Each house was independent and they settled all over England, in small towns, large cities, or in very remote places.

The Augustinians were also known as Black Canons. Their houses were generally Priories although a few were Abbeys.

PREMONSTRATENSIANS

This Order was founded by St Norbet. He was an aristocrat who gave up a secular career to become a preacher. People started following him and in 1120 he was given a site for a monastery in a forest near Laon.

The house was known as Premontre and its inmates Premonstratensians. They lived in remote places like the Cistercians and performed no parochial duties.

Their habit like the Cistercians was white and they became known as the 'White Canons.'

The first English Abbey of Premonstratensians was founded at Newhouse in Lincolnshire in 1143.

They always lived in Abbeys. They owed allegiance to the Abbey of Premontre.

THE GILBERTINES

The foreign orders of regular canons were joined in 1131, by an English one, the only medieval congregation to originate in this country. This was the order of Sempringham, founded by St Gilbert in the Lincolnshire village of that name.

Gilbert, who was a priest of Sempringham, established seven maidens in a small convent by his church. Lay brethren did the rough outside work for them. In three years Sempringham had been joined by another ten monasteries, with the total being 26.

DOUBLE HOUSES OF GILBERTINE NUNS AND CANONS

Twelve of the Gilbertine houses were called double houses. That is, they had a house of nuns and one of canons in the same precinct, but of course these were strictly separate. These double houses continued until the general suppression. The order was not very rich and the appeal of the order itself was very limited.

In Norfolk there was only one house of Gilbertine Nuns and Canons, this was situated at Shouldham.

They always lived in priories.

NUNS OR CANONESSES

Medieval nunneries were a minor feature of English monastic life. Perhaps medieval society thought on similar lines to those of the ancient Greeks, that women were naturally inferior and that their place was at home and not in the cloister.

Today the majority of Christian monastic houses are of women.

Several Benedictine nunneries, however, were established in England before the Norman Conquest. The Augustinian cannonesses and the first Cistercian nuns appear in the reign of Henry I.

THE TRINITARIANS, c. 1200

The Trinitarians were also known as Red Friars.

They were not a mendicant order though, being allowed to hold endowments, with the revenues being evenly distributed for the support of the brothers, to relieve the poor, etc., and for the ransom of captives.

This order was later known as the Regular Canons of the Holy Trinity.

ORDER OF MATTARINS AND TRINITARIANS, also called the Order of the Holy Trinity and St Victor For the Redemption of Captives.

This order was founded by John de Matta and Felix de Valois, confirmed by Pope Innocent III, c. 1197.

They wore white robes with a Maltese cross in red and blue.

Their possessions were divided into three parts, one for their own subsistence, one for the relief of the poor and the third for the redemption of captives taken by the Turks.

In England there are only seven known houses of this Order, and all these were dedicated to the Holy Trinity.

Later, it became known as the Order of Ingham in this county. The only Trinitarian house was at Ingham, near Stalham.

ORDER OF FRIARS

Like the monks and Canons Regular, the friars lived in a community and took the triple vow of poverty, chastity and obedience. However, they lived a quite different sort of life. Their houses were really headquarters from which they worked. They were mendicants, living by begging and wandering about the country, using as a base any house of their own order.

Generally the friaries were in towns and the object was to reach the outcast and the poor.

Their churches were usually large for a big congregation.

The first Order of Friars was the
FRANCISCAN OR GREY FRIARS, also known as Friars Minors.
These Friars originally came from St Francis of Assium, or Assise a city of the Duchy of Spoleto in Italy.

The seraphical 'father,' so called was born of wealthy parents in 1182, and was brought up in merchandise until, at the age of twenty-two he renounced his inheritance.

He threw away his money and shoes and dressed as a poor Italian shepherd would. This consisted of a coat and a cloak or mantle with a knotted cord or rope around the waist.

He applied himself to draw up a set of Rules, containing not only the three vows of poverty, chastity and obedience but, also others such as 'to live without property in house, place or thing as pilgrims and strangers in this world, and to be obedient to their superiors in all things not contrary to their

[15]

conscience, or to the rules which he has prescribed them.' The name he called his fraternity was that of Minors, not only because they utterly renounced all temporal interest, but from the humility and lowliness of mind which their profession obliged them to cultivate.

They were sometimes called Mendicants, from their subsisting on alms for which they begged as all friars did, hence the name begging friars.

Their habit consisted of a loose grey material reaching to the heels. From the colour of this they were called Grey Friars. Around the waist was a cord or rope.

St Francis established the Rules of his Order and became the first general of it, confirmed by Pope Innocent III and the Lateran Council in 1215.

His church near Assise in Italy was given to him by the Benedictine monks and was the first church and convent of the Franciscan Order.

In 1217, he sent out missionaries to preach the gospel in several different countries, which met with great success. In 1219, he had five thousand Friars following him, so he resolved to extend his mission throughout the whole world. With this in view he ordered nine of his friars to set out for England.

Four clerks and five lay brothers came. In charge was brother Agnellus de Pifa, first minister of the Order in England.

They first settled in Canterbury, then divided themselves up proceeding to London, Oxford and Cambridge. They came to Norwich in 1226. This was the year in which St. Francis their founder died.

DOMINICANS, KNOWN AS BLACK FRIARS

St Dominic founded the Order of Black Friars in 1216. He was born in 1170 and became an Austin Canon at Osma in Spain, where he was made Prior at the age of twenty-four.

[16]

While he was at Osma the problem of heresy broke out in Northern France. Dominic and some of his companions were called in to deal with it. The main purpose of his mission was the exposition and defence of the faith of his church. He perceived that the problem of heresy required radical new methods, which he himself proceeded to develop and thus the Order of St Dominic was evolved.

Dominican life was the life of the whole order and not just of a particular house. Brethren could be moved from one house to another. This Order was the first to give intellectual discipline pride of place and their day allowed much time for study.

They founded houses both at Oxford and Cambridge which became centres of learning. This order became known as the Order of Preachers. They first settled in Oxford in 1221.

The first house in Norwich was founded in 1226.

THE CARMELITES OR WHITE FRIARS

These Friars were called Carmelites as their mother house St Mary was on Mount Carmel. The name White Friars was derived from the colour of their habit.

They were expelled from Mount Carmel in 1238, as a result of the capture by the Saracens. They first came to England in 1240. The first Carmelite Friary in Norfolk was at Burnham Norton, founded in 1241.

Their Rule was founded on that of St Basil and was confirmed by Pope Honorius III in 1224 and again in 1250 by Pope Innocent IV.

THE AUSTIN FRIARS

This Order was formed by the amalgamation of a number of lesser bodies. The Order can be traced back to several groups of semi-eremitical communities of hermits in Italy, who by the twelfth century had almost all adopted the Rule of St Augustine. The Pope intervened in 1256 and made a single Order, which allowed them to be mendicants. They were influenced by the Dominicans and gradually ceased their hermits way of life to become urban and intellectual.

Their foundation was at Clare in Suffolk in 1230. They wore a black habit.

MINOR ORDERS

There were several minor orders of friars in Norfolk with rather colourful names, such as the Priory of the Friars de Saco, or Brethren of the Sac, also called Penitentia Jesu, but they had little support.

Most of the lesser orders of friars were suppressed in 1274. New members were not allowed to enrol from that date, so the order came to a natural end at the death of the inmates.

ALIEN PRIORIES

Alien Priories were cells or small convents established by and generally subordinate to foreign monasteries.

Some were conventual, choosing their own priors, applying the revenues to their own use and benefit, and paying only an acknowledgement to the foreign house. Others were entirely dependant thereon and transmitted the whole of their revenue. For this reason their estates were generally confiscated when war broke out between England and France. Such confiscations took place during the reigns of Edward I, Edward II, Edward III and Richard II.

MILITARY ORDERS

There were two main military Orders, the Templars and the Hospitallers, both were semi-monastic orders.

These two Orders were behind the Crusading movement which from 1099 brought Jerusalem and the surrounding areas temporarily into western hands. Both Orders became very powerful in the Holy Land.

[18]

THE TEMPLARS, OR KNIGHTS OF THE TEMPLE

The Templars originated as an association of knights for the protection of pilgrims to the Holy Land. They rendered a valuable service in this field and soon acquired much property.

Their small houses were known as preceptories, their main ones as Temples.

The main Temple was in London. It was used as an administrative centre, collecting the various moneys from other English houses. Most of the preceptories were small with only a few brethren.

In 1312 the Pope suppressed this Order on various charges. These are recognised to have been mainly faked. The possessions were granted to the Hospitallers. The members who were found not guilty were allowed to join another military Order, or to return to secular life with a pension.

THE HOSPITALLERS, the Knights of the Order of the Hospital of St John of Jerusalem

The Hospitallers originally came from Jerusalem at the end of the eleventh century.

They cared for the sick and protected pilgrims and crusaders. This Order fought to the last in the Holy Land.

In England their head house was at Clerkenwell. The organisation was very similar to the Templars with small houses.

HOSPITALS

Medieval hospitals dealt not only with the sick, but for the aged, the poor and the travellers. They can be divided into a number of groups:

Hospitals for religious orders and the clergy.

Hospitals for the poor, aged and sick, with almshouses hospitals or hospices for pilgrims and poor travellers.

[19]

Leper Hospitals, in the middle of the fourteenth century when leprosy became rare, the hospitals looked after the poor and sick.

The majority were secular, but some were monastic. The social value of the hospitals meant they suffered less severely than the monasteries from the storms of the Reformation.

The Great Hospital, founded in 1249, in Norwich, is still in use, having maintained an unbroken existence from that date.

Gazetteer

ALDEBY PRIORY, NEAR BECCLES   **Benedictine Monks**

The Priory was dedicated to St Mary.

This priory was founded as a cell to the Priory of Norwich, by Agnes, wife of Robert de Rye in about 1100.

There was no monastic church, the monks using the parish church. They maintained the Eastern portion. There is much Norman work remaining in the church, including the doorway.

It was dissolved in 1534 and was valued with Norwich. The property went to Henry VIII.

The Prior, at the Dissolution, was made Prebendary of Norwich Cathedral.

There was an agreement, dated 1310, which allowed the Prior to take marl out of the great common of Aldeby, 'to marle his lands.'

The remains now form part of Priory Farm, Aldeby.

ATTLEBOROUGH   **College and Chantry of Secular Canons**

This College and Chantry was dedicated to the Honour of the Exaltation of the Holy Cross and the Church to the Assumption of the Blessed Virgin Mary.

It was founded by the will of Sir Robert de Mortimer in 1399. At its foundation there was a Master and four secular canons.

[21]

Nothing now remains of the College. It was sited north-west of the churchyard. A building now occupies the site.

At the Dissolution it was valued at £21.16.4d.

It was granted to the Earl of Sussex, who pulled down the chancel of the church and probably removed the screen to the west end. This screen is now back in its original position at the east end.

ATTLEBRIDGE, NEAR REEPHAM   A Hermitage

There was a Hermitage and Chapel in this village.

The site is between the two bridges on the north side of the road which runs between Norwich and Fakenham.

It was in existence up to the time of Henry VIII.

Nothing now remains.

BEESTON REGIS PRIORY, NEAR SHERINGHAM
Canons of the Augustinian Order

Dedicated to St Mary the Virgin.

It was founded by Lady Isabel de Cressey in 1216. This lady endowed the Priory with a manor, certain land services and a fishery.

The income was never very great and it never maintained more than a small number of canons.

At the Dissolution it was valued at £43.2.4¾d.

It was granted to Sir Edmund Wyndham and Giles Seafowle esquire.

There are fairly extensive remains. They lie to the west of Beeston Regis parish church. The church of the Priory is in impressive condition, it was 130 feet long.

BILLINGFORD, NEAR EAST DEREHAM
Hospital and Chapel of St Paul at Bec

This Hospital was dedicated to St Paul and St Thomas of Canterbury.

William de Bec founded and built this hospital in Billing-

[22]

ford for the reception of poor travellers as they passed on their way to Walsingham.

It was started in the first half of the thirteenth century. The patronage was given by the founder to the Bishop of Norwich, in 1224.

It was well endowed with manors and lands, being upwards of thirty parishes in Norfolk.

This hospital consisted of a Master and Chaplains. It provided thirteen beds every night for strangers.

The Master himself had a city residence in Norwich.

At the Dissolution it was valued at £4.15.9d. It was granted to Sir John Perrot.

The site is now occupied by a farmhouse called Beck Hall. The hospital was surrounded by a large rectangular moat.

BINHAM PRIORY, NEAR WALSINGHAM   Benedictine Monks

Dedicated to St Mary.

Before the Norman Conquest, Binham had a freeman named Esket as lord. After the conquest, William I granted Binham to his nephew, Peter de Valoines, Lord of Oxford Castle.

It was here, in 1091, that Peter de Valoines and his wife Albreda, founded a Benedictine Priory, subordinate to St Albans Abbey. It was completed about 1104. It was to pay on St Albans Day, to the parent monastery, a mark of silver.

The Abbot of St Albans was allowed once a year to stay at Binham for eight days and no longer unless invited by the Prior. The number of the monks was not to be less than eight.

The heirs and successors of the founder were to remain patrons and protectors of the cell.

Early in the reign of King John, about 1212, Robert Fitz Walter claimed to be patron of the priory. He was on very friendly terms with the then Prior Thomas. As a result of this friendship the Abbot of St Albans removed the Prior, upon which Fitz Walter produced an alleged deed of patronage, which provided that the Prior of Binham should not be removed without the consent of the patron. Fitz Walter forthwith beseiged the priory causing the monks great hardship. They had to eat bread made of bran and to drink water from the drain pipes.

When King John heard of the siege he is said to have sworn to his usual oath: 'Ho, by God's feet, either I or Fitz Walter must be King in England. Ho, by God's feet, whoever heard of such things in peaceable times in a Christian land.'

He sent an armed force to the relief of the Priory and the siege was raised. Fitz Walter had to flee for his life.

One of the monks, Alexander de Langley, died at Binham on December 26th, 1224. His story is a tragic one.

He was once Prior of Wymondham and then returned to St Albans as the Keeper of the Abbot's Seal. He became known as the great letter writer. Unfortunately, he studied so much he became insane. When the other brethren could put up with his outbursts of frenzy and anger no longer, he was publicly censured in Chapter by the Abbot and flogged, 'to a copious effusion of blood.'

He was then taken to Binham.

The Abbot commanded that this poor monk be kept in fetters in solitary confinement until his death. Even then he was buried at Binham in his chains.

He is said to be buried on the North side of the church.

About this time the church of Little Ryburgh paid five marks towards providing wine for the monks of Binham when they were bled. (Many religious houses practised blood-letting at this time). It also provided that on those days when the monks of Binham did not have gruel or cheese by custom, they were to be furnished by the church of Ryburgh.

In 1317, William de Somerton was appointed as Prior.

He was very interested in the study of alchemy and spent vast sums in this pursuit, thus impoverishing the Priory.

He sold two good chalices, which were worth more than all

the other chalices put together, plus six copes, three chasubles, silk cloths and seven gold rings. Not only that, he sold cups and spoons. He even sold the silver cup and crown which was suspended before the Great Altar.

When the Abbot tried to visit his cell at Binham he was forcibly stopped by the Prior, helped by the Earl of Leicester and Sir Robert Walpole.

The Abbot appealed to Edward II, who issued a writ for the arrest of the Prior and his monks who at that time numbered thirteen.

The Prior himself fled to Rome. Six of his monks were taken to the Abbey of St Alban and for a time imprisoned there. This was in 1321.

After a time the Prior returned to England. At the request of his powerful friends he was reinstated as Prior again.

In 1335, he was forced again to flee from Binham. This time he left the Priory in debt to the sum of over £600. A sizeable fortune in those days.

Prior William Dyxwell who was appointed in 1461, was another colourful character.

The Abbot of St Albans, on January 7th, 1463, applied to Edward IV, for means to arrest Prior Dyxwell as he 'like another son of perdition, he goes about from place to place, from town to town, and from market to market more like a vagabond and an apostate than a regular monk and producing in his travels the greatest scandel to the Order as to the religion in general.'

So Prior Dyxwell was deposed, but in 1465, he was re-appointed Prior and seven years later he received the appointment for life.

The Priory was dissolved in 1540, after a visit by one of Cromwell's visitors, Sir Robert Ryche.

In an existing letter to Cromwell, Sir Robert writes 'My lord, I entend to suppress Bynham before my return, which pretendyth itself to be a Sell to Seynt Albans, yf ye advertyse me not to the contrary. I have fynes and other matters of record levyed by them not namyng the Abbot of Seynt Albanys; also contynually they make leases under their owne seale, not namyng the Abbott.'

At the suppression there were only six monks and the total revenues were about £150. The site and possessions of the Priory were granted to Thomas Paston, fifth son of Sir William Paston.

The ruins are very extensive and much restoration has been done. The church has also been restored and is in regular use.

BLACKBOROUGH NUNNERY (MIDDLETON)

Benedictine Nuns

This Nunnery was dedicated to the honour of the Blessed Virgin Mary and St Catherine.

This was originally a Priory founded by Sir Roger de Scales and his wife Muriel in the reign of King Stephen. It was for religious persons of both sexes.

Robert de Scales, son of the founder, settled it upon nuns of the Benedictine Order sometime before 1200. Sir Roger endowed it with various revenues and estates, further augmented by other benefactors, with the churches of Islington, Raynham St Martin, Bircham Parva and Middleton, all in Norfolk. Also of Pansworth in Cambridgeshire and Wetherden in Suffolk with lands, manors and tithes in fifteen parishes.

Two Bishops appear among the list of benefactors, Walter de Suffield in 1256, and Bishop Goldwell in 1497.

The nunnery consisted of a Prioress and ten nuns.

It was valued at £42.6.7½d at the Dissolution and was granted to Thomas Thirlby, Bishop of Norwich, and his successors.

At one time in the nunnery the nine Benedictine nuns had

eight women servants and nine men servants in the house, luxury indeed.

In 1834 a skeleton was dug up from the foundations. It was the perfect skeleton of a man 7 feet tall. A stone coffin containing a skeleton was dug up in 1870. This is now in the care of the museum in King's Lynn.

Parts of the building still remain. They adjoin Priory Farm.

BLAKENEY FRIARY   Carmelite Friars

This Friary was dedicated to the honour of God and the Virgin Mary.

It was founded in 1296 by gifts of land from people, including John Stormer, Richard Stormer and Thomas Tholer. They gave 13 acres of land on which to build a church and convent for Carmelite Friars.

Sir William Roos and his wife gave 100 marks towards the building of the church. The building was started about 1295 and completed in 1321.

At the Dissolution it was granted to William Rede, who immediately aliened it to Thomas Gresham.

There are few remains. They lie to the north of St Nicholas church, some distance north of the A road. The remains are incorporated into a later building. They include a buttress and some fragments of a window.

BROMEHILL PRIORY (WEETING)   Augustinian Canons

Dedicated to the Blessed Virgin Mary and St Thomas the Martyr, Archbishop of Canterbury.

Sir Hugh de Plais founded this priory in the reign of King John (1199-1216).

He endowed it with the Manor of Weeting, and the family of Plais for several generations were its patrons and benefactors.

Richard II (1377-1399), in the ninth year of his reign, gave

[27]

to it the church of Abington in Northamptonshire. In 1528, seven manors belonged to this priory.

The priory was suppressed by a Papal Bull of Pope Clement VII, in May 1528. It was given to Cardinal Wolsey for the endowment of his new college at Ipswich.

In 1452 there was only a prior and three canons in residence.

At one time it was the residence of John Shadwell, father of Thomas Shadwell, Poet Laureate under the Commonwealth, who was brought here at the age of 14.

The foundations only remain. They are about half a mile north-east of Brandon station, on the Norfolk side of the Little Ouse.

BROMHOLM (BACTON)   Cluniac Monks
Dedicated to the honour of God, St Mary and St Andrew.

In 1113, William de Glanville founded Bromholm Priory at Bacton near the sea. It was a cell to Castle Acre for seven or eight Cluniac monks. His grant was confirmed by his eldest son Bartholomew de Glanville who also added sums of his own.

The original building was very small, but early in the 13th century a considerable enlargement took place. This can be seen today by examining the fragment remaining against the east wall of the north transept. It is later in style than the wall it abuts upon, but it does not range with the walls of the transept.

At the same time the chapter house and dormitory beyond were built, probably replacing the smaller buildings. This enlargement was due to the Priory guarding a so called valuable relic. It happened thus:

Baldwin, Count of Flanders, was made Emperor of Constantinople, where he reigned for many years. He was always being harassed by the infidel kings, against whom he marched. Before he went into battle he always paraded the 'Cross of

[28]

Our Lord,' and other relics, before him, in front of his enemies. On the last occasion he neglected to take the Cross with him and his carelessness cost him his life.

He rushed upon the enemy with his small army, paying no regard to the multitude of his enemies, with the disastrous outcome that most of his men were killed or taken prisoner.

Count Baldwin himself was taken prisoner at Adrianople on 15th April, 1205, but his own men knew nothing of this and thought he was dead. He was actually killed the following year.

At this time he had a chaplain of English extraction, who, with his clerks, performed divine service in the Emperor's chapel, and he had charge of the Emperor's relics, rings, etc.

When this chaplain heard that his Lord the Emperor had been killed he left the city of Constantinople privately, taking with him all the relics, etc., including the 'Cross of Our Lord.'

He came to England and went to St Albans. He sold to a monk there, a Cross set with silver and gold, plus two fingers of St Margaret and some odd gold rings and jewels. He then drew from his mantle a wooden Cross and showed it to the monk. He declared on oath that it was a piece of the Cross on which the Saviour of the world was suspended for the redemption of the human race.

The monk disbelieved him.

After that he took the Cross to several monasteries and was not believed.

At length he came to the chapel of Bromholm, which was very poor indeed and nearly destitute of buildings. He showed the Prior and the brethren the Cross, which was constructed of two pieces of wood placed across one another. It was nearly as wide as the hand of a man. The Prior and his brethren were overjoyed to receive such a treasure and they, with all due reverence, carried the Cross into the oratory and with all due devotion preserved it there (1223).

In return the chaplain was received into the Order with his two children.

This Cross was the cause of the prosperity of Bromholm. There was of course no reasonable evidence of identity, or even that it was the Cross of Baldwin, but rather unusual things began to happen.

In the year 1223, when the Prior first received the Cross, so called Divine Miracles began to be wrought in the monastery, the dead were restored to life, the blind recovered their sight, the lame their power of walking, the skins of lepers made clean and those possessed of the devils were released from them.

Not only the English came, but people from many different countries, having heard of the power of the Cross.

In 1233, King Henry III, with his court resided here for a short time and confirmed several grants on to the monastery.

In 1298, Pope Celastine V, in his fourth year absolved the priory from all subjection to that of Castleacre.

At the Dissolution it was granted to Sir Thomas Wodehouse of Waxham.

The Paston family were also patrons of the Priory. In 1466, Sir John Paston died in London trying to recover Caister from the Duke of Norfolk, who had seized it.

Sir John was brought from London to Bromholm Priory to be buried. The funeral itself was carried out with great pomp and extravagance. There is an account of the preparations.

For three whole days one man was engaged in flaying beasts. Provision was also made for : thirteen barrels of beer, twenty-seven barrels of ale, one barrel of 'great assye,' (a very strong drink), a runlet of wine of fifteen gallons, plus, five coombs of malt at one time and ten at another were brewed up for this occasion. The country all around was swept for geese and chickens. With the above went : 1,300 eggs, 20 gallons of milk and eight of cream, plus, 41 pigs, 49 calves and 10 'nete' slain.

Many pounds of wax went to make candles to burn over the

grave. £20 in gold was changed into small coins, 'for showering among the attendant throng.'

A barber was engaged for five days to smarten up the monks for the ceremony.

The priory glazier had to remove two panes of glass to allow the fumes to escape, 'lest the congregation should be suffocated.'

The Prior had a cope made of a 'frogge of worstede' presented to him on the occasion, and the tomb was covered with a cloth of gold.

According to Capgrave, 19 blind men had their sight restored and 39 people were raised from the dead by the 'Cross of Our Lord.'

There are extensive remains still standing.

The church was 200 feet long and 50 feet wide with transepts 90 feet across.

In 1317 the Prior bought a house in All Saints' Green in Norwich and turned it into an inn called the Holy Cross of Bromholm. Here the members and others of their order were entertained.

BUCKENHAM, OLD PRIORY   **Black Canons of St Austin**
Dedicated to St Mary and St James and All Saints.

It was founded in 1146, by William d'Albini, second Earl of Arundel and Chichester. His father founded Wymondham Abbey.

William d'Albini gave the monks the site of Buckenham Castle, which was destroyed, and eighty acres of land.

It must have been a very prosperous Priory in its time, although obscure. They had in the Priory church, five silver-gilt crosses, one silver-gilt pix, two silver candlesticks, a silver-gilt ship, two parcel gilt basons, and a parcel gilt censer. One cope of red velvet, two copes of blue velvet, three copes of white damask, one of red, one of red satin, one of blue satin, two of white satin and four of white fustian.

[31]

At one time there were five Austin canons in residence. They had twenty-one waiting servants. Also as officers, a steward of the court, a hayward, a woodward, and a porter, also a cellarer chosen from the canons.

The canons yearly distributed in charity the equivalent of the rent of one hundred acres of land.

At the Dissolution it was granted to Sir Thomas Knevet of Buckenham Castle. It was valued at £108.10.2¼d.

The remains are south-west to the remains of the castle.

BUCKENHAM (OLD)   Cell and Chapel

This Cell was dedicated to St Mary.

It was built after the foundation of the castle, partly parochial, partly monastic, by the Lords of Buckenham.

At the west end of the chapel was a monastic cell.

At the Dissolution it was granted to Sir Thomas Knevet.

The remains are still in existence, but are now used as a barn.

There were two castles at Buckenham. The first was destroyed and the site was given to the Black Canons of St Austin by William d'Albini. This was at Old Buckenham. The later castle, with Cell and Chapel, was built near the earthworks at New Buckenham.

BURGH ST PETER PRIORY, NEAR BECCLES

Near St Mary's church are the slight remains of a medieval building. It is sometimes referred to as the Priory of St John.

BURNHAM NORTON, NEAR WELLS   Carmelite Friary

Dedicated to the Virgin Mary.

The Friary was founded in 1241, by Sir William de Calthorpe of Burnham Thorpe and Sir Roger de Hemenshale, Lord of Polstead Manor in Burnham. This is thought to be the first foundation of the Carmelites or White Friars in Norfolk.

Robert Bale, author of the 'Chronicle of the Carmelite

[32]

Order,' was born at Bale, near Walsingham. He was at first a novice at Norwich and spent part of each year studying at the Carmelite houses in Oxford and Cambridge. He was later made Prior of Burnham.

When he died in 1503, he left a valuable library to Burnham Norton Friary.

At the Dissolution it was granted to William Lord Cobham and was valued at £1.10.8½d. At this time (1538), it owned 68 acres of land. The plate consisted of 3 ozs. of guilt, 58 ozs. of white and a nutt garnished with silver.

In May 1538, Lady Anne Calthorpe of Polstead Manor wrote to Cromwell the Vicar General, asking if she could buy the Friary. She said there were only four Friars left who were too poor to keep the house in repair and wished to sell it. She said she had one poor dwelling house in Norwich where she was often driven by the plague. The request was not granted at that time.

She did actually buy the Friary in 1554, but only kept it one year, selling it to William Blennerhasset and his wife Anne.

Later on it passed to the Pepys family, relatives of the diarist Samuel. It now belongs to Lord Leicester, of Holkham Hall, near Wells.

The gatehouse still remains, also a portion of the west end of the Friary. The foundations can still be traced.

BURNHAM THORPE, NEAR WELLS — Monastic Chapel

There was once a Monastic Chapel here, founded in 1229. At some time it was given by Walter de Grancourt to Lewes Priory in Sussex.

It was dissolved before 1500.

Nothing remains above the foundations.

CAISTER-NEXT YARMOUTH — College and Chapel

Trinity College and Free Chapel, and St. Margaret's Chapel and College.

In 1459, Sir John Fastolff founded the College of St Margaret, for seven priests and seven poor people. Before this there was a free chapel attached to the manor house in the reign of Edward I, and dedicated to the Holy Trinity and St John the Baptist. This earlier foundation was also supposed to have been a college.

Both foundations were on the same site.

The first foundation was outside the area enclosed by the moat of Caister Castle.

The later foundation of St Margaret's College was inside the area of the moat, as the moat itself had been enlarged at this time.

It was dissolved in 1548 and granted to Sir William Paston.

The remains of the castle built by Sir John Fastolff 1432-5, still exist as does the moat.

To the south of the castle, outside the moat, many human bones have been brought up from time to time.

CARBROOK MAGNA, NEAR WATTON

Commandery and Chapel of Knights Hospitalers

This Commandery was founded by Roger, Earl of Clare, in 1173.

In 1182, his widow, Maud, Countess of Clare, gave the preceptory of Carbrook to the Knights Hospitalers, endowing it with the advowsons of Great and Little Carbrook, and more than half of those parishes.

These gifts were confirmed by her son Richard de Clare, Earl of Hertford, and King John in 1199. From this time, Maud, Countess of Clare, was styled the foundress.

At the Dissolution it was valued at £65.2.11d and granted to Sir Richard Gresham and Sir Richard Southwell.

In the church there are 16 stalls for the use of a Prior and 15 knights.

Nothing now exists of the original buildings.

CARBROOK PARVA, NEAR WATTON
Commandery of Sisters Hospitalers

This Commandery was founded by Maud, Countess of Clare, in the early part of the reign of Henry II. Some of the Sisters of the Order were placed in a hospital near the parish church of St John the Baptist.

In 1180, King Henry II gave the monastery at Buckland in Somerset to the Knights Hospitalers on the condition that all the Sisters of the Order should be placed therein.

Thus Buckland became the only house in England of this Order.

When the nuns and Sisters of Carbrook Parva went to Buckland, the parish was charged from that time with an annual payment of 13/4d towards their support.

Nothing remains above the foundations.

The church of St John was pulled down in 1424.

CARROW NUNNERY, NORWICH   Benedictine Nuns

The Nunnery was dedicated to the Virgin Mary and St John.

On the site, which was once a distinct parish, was a parochial church dedicated to St James the Apostle, before whose image there was a light burning during divine service.

At the west door stood an image of St Christopher. It was still in use in 1520 and served by parochial chaplains, appointed by the Prioress, who paid them for their services.

The ancient hospital or nunnery was dedicated to Mary and St John. To this nunnery King Stephen bestowed all the uncultivated land in Norwich field and all the meadows between Ber Street Gate to Trowse Bridge.

Thus being endowed, two sisters of this community refounded a new monastery in 1146. These sisters were known at Seyma and Leftelina. At the same time King Stephen founded the conventual church of St Mary and made the whole parish an exempt jurisdiction belonging to the Prioress. The site within the walls contained about ten acres.

It was to consist of a Prioress and nine Benedictine black nuns, afterwards increased to twelve.

In 1199, King John granted the nuns a liberty of holding a fair for four successive days at their village.

In 1273, the Pope forbade their receiving more nuns than they could maintain. This was after a representation to him that the English nobility were pressing them to take more sisters than they could support.

The nunnery was also a school or place of education for young ladies, who boarded with and were educated by the nuns.

In 1291, the nunnery was very prosperous with possessions in 75 parishes in Norfolk alone. At the Dissolution the revenues and property were valued at £123.8.5d, most of this going to John Shelton.

The last Prioress, Isabel Wygum, built herself a most magnificent house to the west of the cloisters. It still remains in part. If one looks at this sumptuous house, perhaps it justifies the Dissolution.

This is part of a record of a visit to Carrow by a pre-Reformation Bishop: 'The nuns of the Benedictine Priory complain that their beer is weak. One of the complainants was over eighty years old.'

One side of the nunnery is bounded by the river. At one time this river abounded with perch, tench, roach, dace, gudgeons, bream, ruffs, eels, etc., and sometimes salmon.

The remains have been converted into a beautiful residence surrounded by gardens. It belongs to the Coleman family and is occasionally open to the public.

CASTLE ACRE   Cluniac Monks

Dedicated to St Mary the Virgin.

The Cluniac Priory of Castle Acre was founded by the second Earl of Surrey, William de Warenne, as a cell to the Priory of Lewes in Sussex. It was his father, the first Earl and his wife Gundrada who introduced the Cluniac Order into this country.

The date of the foundation cannot be precisely determined, but it is thought to be about 1090.

The first site proved too small, so the monks moved to the present site occupied by the remains, in the valley of the Nar.

The second Earl confirmed the existing grants and added others, including 15 acres of land and 2,000 eels in Methwold, five shillings rent of land, and one garden, and two acres of land towards the building of the church.

He also gave the monks a serf, Ulmar the stonemason in Acre, so the monks might have skilled assistance in the building of the Church.

The possessions of the monastery increased. Both Henry I and II were benefactors. They granted charters of freedom from toll.

In 1293, the monastery was in debt to the extent of a thousand marks (£666.13.4d) and the Prior of Lewes was instructed to set matters right.

By 1294, the number of monks had excessively diminished and the Prior of Lewes was ordered to see that the house was restored to its ancient and accustomed number.

In 1351, the King had to instruct his Serjeant-at-arms to arrest monks of Castle Acre who had spurned the habit of their order and were living as vagabonds in England in secular habit.

The Priory of Castle Acre had four dependent houses, Bromholm (Bacton), Normansburgh (South Rainham), Slevesholm (Methwold), all in Norfolk, and Mendham in Suffolk.

They were all subject to the mother house, to which they made a small annual payment.

In the middle of the 15th century there appears to have been about 26 monks, but sometimes there were thirty or more.

At the Dissolution there were ten monks in residence. In

[37]

1533 the clear revenue of the monastery was £306.11.4¾d.

Thomas Malling, the last Prior, surrendered the Priory with the Manor of Castle Acre to Henry VIII on 22nd November, 1537. The Prior and ten monks signed the deed.

The property was granted to Thomas Howard, Duke of Norfolk.

The remains are extensive, being enclosed with a wall of flint. The area covers about 30 acres. It is now cared for by the Ministry of Works.

At this Priory was exhibited the so-called arm of St Philip, being the most valuable relic they possessed. In 1533 the sum derived from the exhibition of this arm was 10/-, that is for the year.

CHOSELEY, NEAR DOCKING
Preceptory or Hospital for Brethren of the Order of Jerusalem
Dedicated to St Lazarus, but the brethren probably obeyed the Rule of St Augustine.

This was a Preceptory or Hospital for the relief and support of lepers and old and sick members of the military orders.

It was given by Walter Gifford, the second Earl of Buckinghamshire to the brethren of St Lazarus in the Hospital of Burton Lazars in Leicestershire, in the time of Henry I (1100-1135).

The Master or preceptor of this hospital resided here and accounted to the Master of Burton Lazars Hospital, which was dependent on the great house in Jerusalem. This Master took care of the property of the Order in this part of the county.

At the Dissolution it was valued at £11.4.11d.

In 1544 it was granted to Sir John Dudley, Viscount Lisle.

Nothing remains above the foundations.

Its site is near the outbuildings of Chosely Farm. It is a very isolated part of the country.

CLAXTON, NEAR LODDON   Monastic Chapel and Chantry
This Chapel was dedicated to St Mary.

[38]

The origin is unknown, but it was in use in 1352.

It was for a Master and Chaplains.

The site is near the remains of Claxton Castle. This was originally a manor house which Walter de Kerdiston turned into a castle sometime in the reign of Edward III (1327-1377).

Nothing now remains.

CLAXTON, NEAR LODDON   Monastic Chapel

This Chapel was dedicated to St John the Baptist.

It was in use in 1485.

Nothing remains above the foundations. It was sited near St Andrew's church.

COXFORD PRIORY (EAST RUDHAM)   Augustinian Canons

The Priory was dedicated to the Blessed Virgin Mary. A chapel in the Priory was dedicated to St Radegund. There was also a Guild dedicated to St Radegund.

Early in the reign of King Stephen (1135-1154), William de Cheney founded in the church of St Mary at East Rudham, a Priory of regular canons of the Order of St Augustine. At the beginning of Henry III's reign (1216-1272), they were removed to the eastern edge of the parish, to Coxford.

There were many benefactors, many being titled.

In 1291 it had rents in 42 parishes in Norfolk. Just before the Dissolution it claimed an interest in 11 churches, 5 manors and 44 parishes.

In 1526 an anchoress resided in an outbuilding of the Priory.

In 1534 its value was in the region of £122. It was granted to Thomas Howard in 1537.

There are remains to be seen, consisting of parts of walls and one window archway. There seems to have been a moat at one time.

The site is on meadow land, on the left of the road from East Rudham to Broomsthorpe.

In 1281 it was reported: 'That the canons chatted up the girls and hunted too much.'

CRABHOUSE NUNNERY
(WIGGENHALL ST MARY MAGDALEN)   Augustinian Nuns

The Nunnery was dedicated to SS Mary Magdalen, John the Evangelist and Thomas and Peter.

Roger, the Prior of Normansburgh (South Raynham), with the consent of William de Lisewise, Lord of the site and founder of Normansburgh Priory about 1181, granted to a nun called Lena, a hermitage in a solitary place, in Wiggenhall St Mary Magdalen.

The grant of the site was confirmed by Godfrey Lisewise (son of the above), to the Priory of Castleacre as the principal house.

There were many benefactors including Bishop Goldwell of Norwich, in 1497.

The nunnery consisted of a Prioress and seven nuns.

Lena the first nun was the daughter of Godric de Lynn.

The value of the nunnery in 1534 was £24.19.6d, consisting of property in 13 parishes.

Numerous objects have been found from time to time around the site, objects such as urns, a stone axe, bronze blades, bones, etc. This could be because the nunnery stands on the only piece of land which stood high and dry during the fen floods.

The Augustinian nuns at this nunnery were of the Order of Fontevrault.

Immorality was rare in Norfolk's female religious houses, but here at Crabhouse, there was one case of a nun committing 'an immoral act'. This was the first case for over 40 years.

CREAKE (NORTH) ABBEY   Augustinian Canons

This Abbey was dedicated to St Mary.

Sir Robert de Narford, Governor of Dover Castle, and his

wife Alice, founded at North Creake, in 1206, a hospital and church dedicated to St Bartholomew, for a Master, 4 chaplains and 13 lay brethren.

The first Master, with the consent of Lady Alice, soon became a Prior of the Order of St Augustine.

In 1230, Lady Alice granted the patronage of the Priory to Henry III. He immediately turned it into an Abbey. This is one Abbey that Henry VIII did not dissolve, for in 1504, every canon died of the plague in one week. The income of the Abbey went to Christ's College in Cambridge.

Christ's College itself was founded in 1506 by Lady Margaret, Countess of Richmond and Derby. This Lady was mother of Henry VII.

In North Creake church is a fine brass to William Calthorpe in academical dress holding a church on his arm. This is thought to have been taken from Creake Abbey when it was dissolved. William Calthorpe was a benefactor to the Abbey.

The accounts show that in 1345 two knives value $1\frac{1}{2}$d. were given to two girls for bringing apples to the Abbot. Chaucer, who was born in Lynn, says of the Prior: 'His tippet was aye stuffed full of knives. And pins to give fair wives.'

The remains are of great interest and are maintained by the Ministry of Works.

CROXTON HOSPITAL (FAKENHAM)   **Chapel and Hospital**

This Chapel and small hospital was founded at Croxton near Fulmodeston in 1250.

The land was given by Richard de Surrie and his wife Sarah.

It was a branch of the larger hospital at Thetford, and there were only two or three brethren.

At the Dissolution the hospital and land were granted to Sir Richard Fulmerstone, about 1540.

The site was near the parish church of St John the Baptist. The church is in ruins.

CUSTHORPE (WESTACRE)   Cell and Chapel

This Cell or House was dedicated to St Thomas à Becket.

Custhorpe was given by Sir Ralph de Toney as part of the endowment of Westacre Priory. The canons built here a large chapel, to the north-east was a cell or house, in which some canons from Westacre dwelt and performed the services in the chapel.

Every year there was an annual fair held at Custhorpe on the anniversary of the translation of St. Thomas à Becket. This was granted in 1479 by Edward VI.

Many pilgrims visited this chapel when on the their way to Walsingham. It seems likely that a relic of St Thomas was preserved here.

In the early 1500's it consisted of a Master and three canons.

At the Dissolution it was valued with Westacre, both being granted to the Duchess of Richmond.

The remains of the chapel can be seen on the north side of the trackway leading from Westacre to Southacre.

DEREHAM (EAST)   Saxon Nunnery

Anna, King of the East Anglians, founded a Nunnery here for his daughter Withburga. She became the first Abbess and died in 654. This makes Dereham one of the oldest churches of royal foundation in the country.

St Withburga was the Superior of a community of virgins.

The house was totally destroyed by the Danes in the raid of 870.

St Withburga's well, which is still in existence, is sited outside the west end of the church.

In 974 the monks of Ely stole the body of the Princess and carried it off to their own monastery and enshrined it there. She has never been brought back.

At some time a Guild of St Withburga was founded here. At the Dissolution it was granted to Thomas Woodhouse.

Nothing remains of the nunnery. The church was made parochial in 798, although nothing remains of this.

The later church, which is still standing and in use, has two towers. There is a 14th century lantern tower in the centre of the church and a completely separate bell tower.

The spring (St Withburga's Well) is covered by an arch, and is worth a visit. In front of the well can be seen an early stone coffin lid.

DEREHAM (WEST)   **Premonstratension Abbey**

This Abbey was dedicated to the Honour of God and the Blessed Virgin Mary.

It was founded by the then Dean of York, Hubert Walter in 1188.

King John favoured this Abbey and granted to it several privileges. He also confirmed the benefactions of many others.

The monastery had the patronage of, or interest in, 14 churches, with eight manors and revenues in 38 parishes.

The canons that came to this Abbey were brought from the Premonstratension Abbey of Welbeck in Nottinghamshire.

At the Dissolution it was valued at £252.12.11½d. In 1540 the site was granted to Thomas Dereham. He also received a portion of the endowment.

The Lordships remained in the Crown until 1553. They were then granted to Sir Thomas Lovell of East Harling, who conveyed them in turn to Thomas Dereham, son of the above.

There is nothing left above the foundations, these can be traced although covered by grass.

The Dean of York and founder of the Abbey, progressed to become the Bishop of Salisbury, Archbishop of Canterbury, Legate to the Pope, Lord Chancellor and Chief Justice of England, Custis of Windsor Castle and forest, one of the Barons of the Exchequer and Prime Minister of Richard I and Prime Minister of King John.

[43]

DOCKING PRIORY, NEAR HUNSTANTON   Alien

This Priory was for monks from the Abbey of Ibrerio or Yvry, which was in the diocese of Evreaux in Normandy.

It was endowed with tithes in Heacham, Southmere and Titchwell, also with the rectories of Docking and Southmere.

John Lord Lovell was a benefactor of this Priory. It was suppressed in 1415 by the Parliament of Leicester. It was granted to Joan, the Queen Dowager of England, and in 1440 became the property of the provost and fellows of Eton College. They still possess certain lands in Docking.

This Priory was supposed to have been connected to St Mary's Church, but nothing remains.

ELMHAM (NORTH), NEAR EAST DEREHAM

Saxon Cathedral Church

This was the Cathedral church of the See from 673 to 1070. It was then moved to Thetford.

This was not a monastic church, but remained as a cell to the Mother Church of the diocese after 1070.

The church itself was just over 100 feet long with a west tower, nave, transepts with small towers and a semi-circular apse at the east end.

There are extensive ruins, which are maintained by the Ministry of Works.

The Bishops of the Diocese lived here in a palace near the church for some time after the removal of the See.

FIELD DALLING PRIORY, NEAR BINHAM   Cistercian Monks

In the reign of Henry II, Maud de Harscolye (Harscove) gave to the Abbey of Savigny in Normandy a manor at Field Dalling. Some monks from that Abbey settled here in a cell or Priory.

In 1265 Simon de Walton, Bishop of Norwich, confirmed a portion of the tithe.

It was suppressed in 1415 by the Parliament of Leicester and given first to Epworth Priory then to Spital-on-the-Street, Lincolnshire. King Richard gave it to the Carthusians near Coventry. It then passed to Mountgrace Priory in Yorkshire.

In 1555, it was granted to Martyn Hastyngs and James Borne.

The site is now occupied by Manor Farm House.

FLITCHAM PRIORY, NEAR KING'S LYNN

Augustinian Canons

The Priory was dedicated to the Blessed Virgin Mary and was a cell to Walsingham Priory.

It was founded by Sir Robert Aiguillon in the reign of Henry III. In 1370 there were six canons in residence.

From 1316 to 1534 the vicars of the parochial church here were presented by the Prior and convent of St Mary, Flitcham.

At the Dissolution it was valued at £62.10.6½d. and granted to Edward Lord Clinton.

The site is now occupied by the premises of the Abbey Farmhouse.

St Mary's church is said to occupy the site of one built in 600 AD by Bishop Felix.

GAYTON PRIORY, NEAR KING'S LYNN
Alien

This Priory was a Cell to the Abbey of St Stephen at Caen in Normandy.

It was founded by William de Eschoies in 1081. He gave the lordship of Welle to the mother Abbey at Caen.

King William Rufus (1087-1100), Henry II (1154-1189) and Richard I (1189-1199) were listed among the benefactors.

In 1339, as this was part of a foreign monastery, it was seized by the Crown and granted in 1373 to Sir Hugh Fastolff for his life, in 1381 it went to Sir Devereux and his wife Mary, and in 1415 to John Wodehouse.

[45]

In 1468 the property went to the Crown again. In the same year it was granted to St Stephen's College at Westminster. This College was dissolved in 1548. Gayton Priory was then granted to Osbert Mundeford and Thomas Gandy.

Nothing remains, the site being partly occupied by Well Hall.

GAYWOOD HOSPITAL (KING'S LYNN) Hospital

This Hospital was dedicated to the Honour of God and St Mary Magdalen.

It was founded in 1145 by Peter de Chaplain for a Prior and twelve brothers and sisters.

They were governed by rules confirmed in 1174 by the founder and the Archbishops of York and Canterbury.

Many people contributed to this hospital on the condition that their souls would be prayed for by the fraternity.

There were endowments in several parishes in all amounting to 305 acres.

In 1547 the hospital went to the Crown.

In 1611 the hospital was re-founded by the Mayor and Corporation of King's Lynn.

The hospital is now under the control of the Charity Trustees.

GRESSENHALL, NEAR EAST DEREHAM (ROUGHOLM)
College and Chapel

The College and Chapel was dedicated to St Nicholas the Bishop.

The lord of Gressenhall, William de Stutevil, founded this college and chapel in the time of Henry III (1216-72). He endowed it with the manor of Rowholm and with various lands in nine parishes.

The college was governed by a Master who with the brethren lived just south of the chapel.

[46]

In 1534 William Hastings was Master, and at this time it was valued at £12.0.3½d.

It was dissolved in 1550 by Edward VI, and was granted to Sir Nicholas le Strange.

In the early part of the reign of Henry VIII the chapel was used for parochial purposes as well as collegiate.

The ruins were converted into a house.

The site is in the Rougham part of Gressenhall.

GUTHLAC'S STOW, SWAFFHAM   Cell and Chapel

Dedicated to St Guthlac.

Alan de Swaffham, in the reign of Henry II (1154-1189), gave land to the monks of Castleacre, at Stow or Guthlac's Stow, a hamlet at Swaffham.

In a short time after the addition of several endowments the Prior of Castleacre had to find a priest to officiate in the chapel of St. Guthlac twice a week. The benefactors included Alan, Earl of Richmond, and Gilbert de Gaunt, Earl of Lincoln.

The chapel is known to have been in use in 1464, but nothing is known for certain after that.

The site is on the north side of the Narford road, about one mile west of Swaffham. Nothing now remains.

HADDISCOE PRECEPTORY, NEAR LODDON

Knights Templars

The founder of this preceptory is unknown.

It was, however, known to be in existence in 1218. King Henry III (1216-1272) did give a considerable amount of money to it.

The Order of the Templars was abolished in 1312 and their lands forfeited. It is known that this preceptory was in the custody of Thomas de St Omer, Sheriff of Norfolk and Suffolk, in 1326, and passed on to his successor. After that nothing is known.

The site was near St Mary's church. Nothing now remains.

[47]

HAUTBOIS (GREAT), NEAR COLTISHALL

Hospital and Chapel

This Hospital was founded for the reception of travellers and poor people by Sir Peter de Alto Bosco (or Hautbois) about 1235. Sir Peter was steward and procurator to the monastery of St Benet.

It was endowed with lands, rents and services in several adjoining parishes.

The custody of the house was committed to the Master of the Hospital of St James at Holm, under the guardianship of the almoner of St Benet's Abbey.

The hospital had a chapel, bell and chaplain for the use of the brethren, who were to pray for the souls of the founder and his ancestors.

It consisted of a Master and several poor people.

At the Dissolution in 1534 it was valued at $18/7\frac{1}{2}$d. It was dissolved in 1557 by Edward VI, and granted to Thomas Woodhouse of Waxham.

There are no remains above the foundations.

HAVERINGLAND OR MOUNTJOY PRIORY, NEAR CAWSTON

Augustinian Canons

The Chapel was dedicated to St Lawrence.

At first there was a chapel here, founded by William de Gyney, Lord of Haverland. He gave it to the Prior of Wymondham Priory, who was to keep two or three of their monks here.

Early in the reign of King John (1199-1216), William de Gyney founded a priory for Augustinian canons.

Pope Clement IV, in 1264, granted a licence for the Prior and brethren to hold all their lands exempt from tithes.

Pope Urban V favoured this Priory also, and in 1364 took it under his protection.

The rectories of Irmingland, Haveringland and Stanfield (Suffolk) were appropriated to this Priory.

[48]

There were many benefactors, including several knights and nobles.

The Priory itself was dedicated to the Virgin Mary, St Michael and St Lawrence.

It was suppressed in 1528 by Pope Clement. The endowments went to Cardinal Wolsey's College at Ipswich.

The site is just east of Abbey Farm. The Farm itself is approximately one mile south-west of St Peter's church.

The site is surrounded by a moat and some of the foundations can be traced.

HEACHAM PRIORY, NEAR HUNSTANTON — Cluniac Monks

This was a Cell to the monastery of St Pancras at Lewes, which was founded by William de Warenne, First Earl of Surrey. He came to England with William the Conqueror and died in 1088. It seems that a few of the monks lived here at Heacham.

To the Cell were appropriated the rectory, the patronage of the vicarage and the priory manor.

St Mary's parish church was appropriated by the Priory. The transepts of St Mary's have now gone to decay, together with the monastic buildings.

In 1291 the valuation was £75.0.9½d., a considerable amount.

The monastic property was granted to Thomas Howard, Duke of Norfolk, in 1537. St Mary's church is well maintained and still in use.

HELLESDON COLLEGE AND CHANTRY, NEAR NORWICH

John Churchman, Sheriff of London, was executor in 1385 of John de Haylesdone's will. He had a patent for founding a chantry for two chaplains to pray in the church of St. Mary of Haylesdon, for the souls of the said John de Haylesdon and Joan his wife and also Walter de Berney. It was called the 'College of Priests at Haylesdon.'

It was endowed with lands, rents, etc., in several parishes in London and Norfolk.

In 1385, each priest received a portion valued at £6.13.10d., a huge sum in those days.

Sir John Fastolff was a patron mentioned in 1447.

At the Dissolution, each priest was granted a pension of £6 per annum.

The parish church of St Mary's remains and is still in use. Nothing else is to be seen, other than an ancient cross which stands in the churchyard.

HEMPTON PRIORY, NEAR FAKENHAM   **Augustinian Canons**

The Hospital was dedicated to St Mary and St Stephen. The Priory was dedicated to St Stephen only.

This was originally founded as a hospital by Roger de St Martin, Lord of Hempton, in the reign of Henry I (1100-1135). Soon after it was changed into an Augustinian Priory.

It was endowed with the rectory of Hempton, the manors of Hempton, Tofts and Waterden, with lands in several parishes.

The sheep had the liberty of the priory manor.

At the Dissolution in 1534, there was a prior and three canons. They all subscribed to the King's supremacy. At this time it was valued at approximately £35.

In 1545 the site of the priory and land were appropriated to Sir William Farmer and his wife Lady Catherine.

It seems whoever took possession of this priory after its dissolution suffered misfortunes.

The foundations still remain just south of Abbey Farm.

There were never many canons living here but they certainly lived well. Perhaps the Priory deserved to be dissolved. At one time, four canons had 'fifteen servants, ten hinds and five waiting servants.' At the same time the house owned 165 acres of corn land, 13 plough horses, 25 pigs, 5 hine and 165 sheep and lambs.

They certainly had variety at their meals. The Bursar's accounts for a period still remain : 1st week – beef, mutton, eggs, sucking pig, oysters, fresh fish. 3rd week – wild fowl, veal, beef, mutton, fresh herring, fresh fish, salt fish, oysters, eggs and a 'paunch.' Other weeks included – rabbit, smelts, honey, lamb, cockell, chicken and mackeral. At Lent there were raisins and currants and oil, plus salt fish, shad, salmon, turbot, fresh pickeral and mussels. On top of this the condiments, ginger, orris root, cinnamon, saffron and cumia, and one pound of sugar.

HERRINGBY HOSPITAL AND COLLEGE, NEAR ACLE

The church was dedicated to St Ethelbert. It was both collegiate and parochial.

A hospital or almshouse was founded here in 1475 by will on the death of Hugh Atte Fenne.

It was endowed with £44 per annum and the living of the church of Herringby.

The hospital was for a Master, three priests, eight poor people and two servants.

After the Dissolution the church was still used for parochial purposes for a time. Then the living was joined with that of Stokesby.

At the Dissolution in 1534 it was valued at £23.6.5d. In 1545 it was granted to Sir Thomas Clere of Stokesby.

The remains are sited in the private grounds of Herringby Hall. They consist of small portions of the church and of the hospital buildings.

HICKLING PRIORY, NEAR STALHAM   Augustinian Canons

The Priory was dedicated to the Virgin Mary, St Augustine and All Saints.

It was founded in 1185 by Theobald de Valentia, who endowed it with several churches. At this time it was for a Prior and ten canons. There were several benefactors whose gifts were confirmed by King John in 1203. The monastery possessed eight lordships, with the advowsons, portions or vicarages of nine churches.

The last Prior was Robert Botyld (1503), and he subscribed to the King's supremacy in 1534.

It was valued at £100.18.7¾d. in 1537, and was settled on the Bishops of Norwich and their successors.

The remains have been turned into farm buildings at Priory Farm.

At the Dissolution it had possessions in 35 parishes.

HILBOROUGH PILGRIM'S CHAPEL, NEAR SWAFFHAM

This Chapel was dedicated to St Margaret.

It was founded in 1207 by Sir John de Caily and was endowed with 100 acres of land.

It was used by pilgrims who used to stop here when on their way to Walsingham.

The chapel was also used for parochial purposes and was a chapel-of-ease to All Saints at Hilborough, the parish church.

The monastic chapel had its own priests.

In 1550 it was dissolved by Edward VI.

The walls of this chapel are still standing.

HILGAY OR MODNEY PRIORY, NEAR DOWNHAM MARKET
Benedictine Monks

The founder and date of foundation are unknown, but it was in existence in 1291 as a Cell to Ramsey Abbey in Huntingdonshire, then valued at £3.18.0d.

At the Dissolution in 1543 it was granted to Robert Hogan.

The site is partly occupied by Modney Hall Farmhouse. There are also slight remains north of the house in the meadow. The river Ouse runs nearby.

HORNING, ST BENET'S ABBET OF HULME

Benedictine Monks

This is a very isolated Abbey.

It was founded by a group of Saxon monks or recluses *c*. 800 AD, their leader was called Suneman. They built a church to St Benedict, but all was destroyed by the Danes in 870, when they swept over the country.

King Cnut (Canute 1016-1035) re-founded a new convent in 1019 for 25 monks under the Rule of St Benedict. The first Abbot of St Benet's was Elsin in 1020.

He had 24 monks here, 12 of whom were sent under the control of Prior Uvius to form a new monastery at Bury St Edmunds.

From the time of the second foundation the revenues and endowments rapidly increased. The principal register contains a list of 1185 royal, papal and other charters, etc., belonging to the monastery with references to 99 parishes, but in 1532 the monastery was said to have been heavily in debt.

In 1535, by virtue of a private Act of Parliament, the revenues of St Benet's were exchanged for those of the old estates of the See, the Abbey was united to the bishopric and the Bishops of Norwich became from that time and still remain to this day, Abbots of St Benet's at Holm.

In the conventual church under the high altar, two saints are buried, St Wolfey, the first hermit at Holm; and St Margaret, who was killed at Hoveton St John in 1170.

Just before the Dissolution, discipline at this Abbey became very slack. We hear that William Bynham kept away from mattins, 'because he was ill.' Yet he was in excellent health and ate and drank like the rest. It was said there were too many dogs in the precincts. The altar cloths were not clean and there was a lack of service for the sick.

In 1440, charitable donations to the poor were given at 2/4d. and 3/4d. for medicines for the sick for the year. Indeed a paltry sum, considering how rich the Abbey was at that time.

[53]

One thing the monks must have excelled in – Winemaking. One year, enough wine was made at St Benet's to sell. It fetched the princely sum of £5.19.2d.

The site is in the marshes near the junction of the rivers Bure and Ant. It is very isolated. The ruined gatehouse is still there. There are also foundations and pieces of wall scattered about. A long length of wall is in the river.

HORNING MEDIEVAL HOSPITAL

Dedicated to St James.

This Hospital was founded by Abbot Daniel of St Benet's in 1153 for poor people of both sexes. It was governed by the Almoner of St Benet's Abbey.

In 1534 it was granted, with St Benet's, to the See of Norwich.

It stood at the head of the causeway which ran across the marshes, on the opposite side of the river to the Abbey. There used to be a bridge here across the river, but after 1534 it was allowed to become dilapidated and nothing now remains of it.

The hospital buildings are now occupied by Horning Hall farmhouse.

The hospital chapel is now a barn belonging to the farmhouse.

HORSHAM ST FAITH'S PRIORY, NEAR NORWICH
Benedictine Monks

The Priory was dedicated to St Faith.

It was founded by Robert Fitzwalter and his wife Sybil in 1105.

Both husband and wife had been on a pilgrimage to Rome as was the custom in those days. On their way home through France they were captured by robbers and imprisoned. They both prayed to God and St Faith, and the saint appeared in a vision, loosened their fetters and brought them out of prison. Fitzwalter and his wife then made their way to the Benedictine

[54]

Abbey of Conches in the diocese of Eureux, where St. Faith was enshrined, and there offered their chains.

The Abbot received them joyfully with great cheer for twelve days. They vowed to build a monastery in their manor at Horsford when they returned. This was to be a Cell of Conches for the worship of God and St Faith. Two monks from the Abbey returned to Horsham with them. It soon prospered, and in 1291 this Priory had possessions in 77 Norfolk parishes yielding an annual income of £78.6.10¼d.

In 1390 this Priory was made denizen and discharged from all subjection to the Abbey of Conque. About this time Thomas de Berthelet was elected Prior by the monks at Horsham. From then on it was recognised as an English Priory.

At the Dissolution in 1537, Richard Southwell was granted Horsham Priory, and all the manors and rectories attached.

The year before, on 18th August, 1536, Richard Southwell had written to Cromwell: 'This house of Saint Feythe now viewed and at a point to be demolished.'

The site is partly occupied by Abbey Farmhouse next to the church of St Mary and St Andrew. The square, walled garden represents the cloister. This is to the north side of the church. The church is well maintained and still in use.

All needy applicants at this priory were given two herrings and a loaf.

HORSHAM ST FAITH'S HOSPITAL, NEAR NORWICH
Knights Templars

This Hospital was founded by Ralph de Granville in the reign of Henry II (1154-1189). He then gave it to the Knights Templars.

In 1163 this hospital was granted to the Priory on the order of the Pope.

In 1544 the hospital was granted to Sir Richard Southwell and Edward Elrington.

[55]

The site is supposed to be within the precincts of St Faith's Priory.

HORSTEAD PRIORY, COLTISHALL   Alien

King William II (1087-1100) gave the manor and advowson of the parish church of Horstead to the Nunnery of the Holy Trinity at Caen in Normandy, which had been founded by his mother, Maud, Queen Consort of King William the Conqueror.

In 1090, a Priory was founded here at Horstead as a Cell to the Norman Nunnery. King Henry I (1100-1135) confirmed his brother's gift.

In 1291 it was valued at £25.9.5¼d., and possessed land in 7 parishes. As it was an alien priory, it was dissolved in 1415, during the reign of Henry V. It was granted to Sir Thomas Erpingham for his lifetime. Later, in 1431, it was granted to complete the foundation of the College of St Mary and St Nicholas in Cambridgeshire (King's College).

The site is not known, but was supposed to have been near the parish church.

There is a moated site approximately 600-700 feet west of the church. This could possibly have housed the Priory.

HOUGHTON ST GILES PILGRIM'S CHAPEL,
NEAR WALSINGHAM

The Chapel was dedicated to St Catherine the patron saint of pilgrims.

It is not known who founded this chapel which was erected *c.* 1380. It is thought to have been founded by the small Benedictine Priory at Horsham St Faith, near Norwich. They appointed the vicar or deputy to serve the parish.

This is the last of the Pilgrim Chapels on the outskirts of Walsingham. There, the pilgrims would, and still do, remove their shoes and walk the last mile barefoot to the Shrine at Walsingham.

Henry VIII was the last King of England to make the pilgrimage. He stayed at Barsham manor and probably walked this last mile barefooted, as many thousands had done before him. Confessions were also heard at this chapel.

This chapel was in ruins for many years. The west side was in fairly good order and in 1934 the whole chapel was rebuilt and restored and is open for worship. Every year there is an annual pilgrimage sponsored by the Guild of Ransom in honour of Our Lady of Walsingham.

It is well worth a visit.

St Giles himself was the hermit of Languedor. He was much venerated in England and the legend of his protecting the hunted hind which took refuge in his cave, earned him in the middle ages a great deal of sentimental devotion. At the present day he is known as the saint with a devotion to animals.

He is represented as a mitred Abbot, with his hind, on rood screens at Hemstead and at Smallborough.

HUNSTANTON PILGRIM'S CHAPEL

The chapel was dedicated to St Edmund the King and Martyr.

The date and founder of this chapel are unknown, but it is thought to have been built during the late Norman period.

It was for the use of pilgrims who used to come to take the healing waters at certain wells. The water is very rich in iron, due to the carstone underneath.

It was also used as a chapel-of-ease to the parochial church at Old Hunstanton (St Mary the Virgin).

After the Dissolution it fell into ruin.

In 1913 these ruins were repaired and the site was laid out as a garden. These are maintained by Hunstanton Urban District Council.

It is well worth a visit, being situated on top of the cliffs, near the lighthouse at Old Hunstanton.

ICKBURGH LEPER HOUSE AND CHAPEL, NEAR BRANDON

Dedicated to St Mary and St Lawrence.

The leper house was founded in the reign of Edward I (1272-1307) by William Barentun.

In 1323 there was a hospital for lepers here. It was given 145 acres of land by the founder and later another 60 acres by John de la Rokele in the reign of Edward III (1327-1377).

The patronage then went to the Bedingfield family until the Dissolution. In 1323 it consisted of a Master, chaplain and brethren; after this a Master, wardens and friars eremites, and so it then became a small priory. These privileges were confirmed by Pope Nicholas V. However, before the Dissolution it had dwindled into a free chapel which was used for parochial purposes.

In 1534 it was valued at £3.7.6d., and was granted to Osbert Mountford of Feltwell, for a sum of money.

The site is in the southern part of Newbrigg parish and has gone to ruins.

INGHAM PRIORY, NEAR STALHAM   Trinitarians

This was the Order of the Holy Trinity and St Victor, for the Redemption of Captives. It was dedicated to St Mary and the Holy Trinity.

The Priory was founded by Sir Miles Stapleton of Bedale in Yorkshire, and his wife Lady Joan, daughter of Sir Oliver de Ingham, in 1360.

Sir Miles obtained a licence for the parish church to be rebuilt and to become partly the church of the priory. Thus the nave remained parochial and the chancel became monastic.

In 1360 Sir Miles placed friars here of the Order, in the parish church, which was then made collegiate.

It soon became very important and was known as the Order of Ingham, and was the only Trinitarian house in the county of Norfolk.

[58]

At first the priory consisted of a Prior, minister or custos, who had the care of the college; a sacrist, who had care of the parishioners and officiated for them in the church appropriated to the college, and two brethren. They were to pray for the souls of Sir Miles and Lady Joan, the King (Edward III) and others.

In 1534 there was a Prior, a sacrist and six brethren.

The priory possessed four manors and four impropriate churches with lands and interests in 20 parishes.

The first Prior was Richard Marleberge and John Pevesey the first sacrist. The last Prior was John Say, who, with Robert Barham and four brethren, refused to recognise Henry VIII as head of the Church. On August 5th, 1534, the Prior was found by the Commissioners guilty of incontinency.

It was granted to Sir William Woodhouse of Waxham and at that time was valued at £61.9.7d. He exchanged it in 1544 for Hickling Priory.

The remains of the priory are scanty. A small cloister can be traced in the arches adjoining the north wall of the church. The village inn is part of the conventual buildings. The church itself is in good state of repair. Adjoining the south aisle was once a chapel dedicated to St Mary.

In 1832, on the north side of the altar where Sir Oliver was supposed to be buried, a complete suit of armour was dug up. There was no sign of a grave or coffin. This armour has gradually disappeared, now only the helmet remains.

Ingham was written as HINCHAM in the Domesday Book, this means 'seated in a meadow.'

KING'S LYNN - PRIORY   Benedictine Monks

The Priory was dedicated to St Mary Magdalen, St Margaret and all maiden saints.

It was founded in 1100 as a cell to the monastery at Norwich, by the first Bishop of Norwich, Herbert de Losinga. He endowed it with the tithes and ecclesiastical dues of the whole town of Lynn, and with various lands and churches in the area. Bishop Herbert placed here a Prior and three monks. In 1448 a Prior, cellerer, pittancier and a camerarius are mentioned.

In the churchyard was a cross at which offerings were made.

At the Dissolution it was valued with Norwich. In 1534 the spiritualities were given as £38.14.4d. The property was granted in 1537, as part of their new endowment, to the Dean and Chapter of Norwich.

The Priory was on the south side of the conventual church of St Margaret, which was both monastic and parochial. Most of the monastic buildings have been pulled down except for a small piece of wall. St Margaret's church itself is well worth a visit and is in a good state of repair, its length is 235 feet.

KING'S LYNN - PRIORY   Dominican Friars
Dedicated to St Dominic.

The Dominican or Black Friars settled in Lynn in 1272.

The Priory was founded by Thomas Gedney and the house was in the patronage of Thomas Earl of Rutland.

Although these were mendicant friars, they did possess land and tenements in Lynn. At the Dissolution they were valued at 18/-. The Prior and brethren signed the surrender in 1539 and the property went to John Eyre.

The site was in Clough Lane in the eastern part of the town. Nothing now remains.

KING'S LYNN - PRIORY   Franciscan Friars
Dedicated to St Francis.

The Priory was founded by Thomas Feltham *c.* 1264. In 1364 they had a patent to enlarge the priory.

In 1538 the monastery was surrendered by the Prior and nine brethren. It was sold by the King to John Eyre. He, in turn, sold it to a priest, who conveyed it to the Corporation.

[60]

The remains consist of an octagonal tower of red brick and stone. It is surrounded by a public garden maintained by the local Corporation. Well worth visiting. The site is between the Theatre Royal and the London Road.

KING'S LYNN - PRIORY   Carmelite Friars

Dedicated to St Mary.

It is uncertain when and by whom this Priory was founded. It is possible that it was Lord Bardolph, Lord Scales and Sir John de Wiggenhall in 1269. Other authorities think it was Thomas Feltham, who also founded the priory of Grey Friars. It seems likely that the White Friars settled here before 1269, for in 1260 William le Breton was listed as a considerable benefactor.

Many people were benefactors to the priory, including Sir Hamon Felton of Litcham in 1379, William Lord Bardolph in 1384, and Sir Robert Howard in 1388.

In 1534 it was valued at £1.15.8d. In 1538 the Prior and ten brethren signed the surrender of the monastery to the King. In 1544 Henry VIII sold the priory and its property to John Eyre. Sometime after this it was sold to the Corporation.

The site was situated in South Lynn, between All Saints' church and the river. Nothing remains except for the gateway, which is in good condition.

KING'S LYNN - PRIORY   Austin Friars

The Austin Friars were given this land by Margaret de Southmere in 1293. She is thought to have founded the Priory also, although there is no documentary evidence of this. The Priory was enlarged in time as people gave gifts of houses adjoining the priory.

In 1498 Henry VII, his Queen, his mother, the Prince of Wales, and his retinue, were received here during their visit to Lynn.

[61]

The Priory was supplied with water from Gaywood, which was brought here by means of an aqueduct. King Richard II gave a licence for this in 1382.

In 1534 the monastery was valued at £1.4.6d. In 1539 the Prior and fourteen brethren signed the surrender to the King. The property was purchased from the King by John Eyre in 1544.

The site was in St. Nicholas' parish, between Austin Street and Chapel Street. It was partly on the site of the Black Horse Inn. Part of the gateway remains.

KING'S LYNN - PRIORY   Friars of the Sack

This was a small Order, which was suppressed in England in 1307. Generally they were obliged to unite with one of the mendicant orders of friars.

The founder is unknown.

When it was suppressed in 1307, Roger de Flegg was Prior. He was also Vicar General of this Order throughout England.

It is not known for certain where the site was. It is possibly near the site of the Greenland Fisheries.

KING'S LYNN   College of Secular Canons

This College was only in existence for 32 years.

It was founded in 1500 by Thomas Thoresby, Mayor of Lynn in 1477, 1482 and 1502.

The College consisted of a Master and twelve priests.

It was suppressed in 1532.

The site was in College Lane, in St Margaret's parish.

There are slight remains.

KING'S LYNN- ST JOHN'S HOSPITAL

Dedicated to St John the Baptist.

The founder of the hospital is unknown. It was in being in the time of Edward I (1272-1307) if not before.

It consisted of a Master and several poor brothers and sisters.

The patronage was originally in the Mayor and burgesses. They were deprived of it by John de Ely, Bishop of Norwich.

The temporals of the hospital consisted in the main of lands in Lynn, Clenchwarton and Hardwick.

In 1369 the Archdeacon of Norwich, William de Swinflet, gave a donation.

At the Dissolution it was valued at £7.6.11½d.

The site is not known.

KING'S LYNN - COWGATE LAZAR HOUSE

The founder and date of foundation are unknown.

In 1432 Stephen Guybon left a legacy to the house of lepers at Cowgate.

It was suppressed at the general Dissolution.

Its situation was somewhere in Cowgate.

KING'S LYNN - WEST LYNN LEPER HOUSE

A leper house once existed in West Lynn, but the date and founder are not known. The site is also unknown.

In 1432, in his will, Stephen Guybon left a sum of money to West Lynn leper house.

KING'S LYNN - HOSPITAL OF ST LAWRENCE

The Hospital was dedicated to St Lawrence.

This was a hospital or lazar house, with a chapel for the use of lepers.

The advowson belonged to Mathias Herlewine in 1318. In 1337 he conveyed it, together with the rents, homages, etc., to Thomas Durrent and others.

John Durrent, in 1448, granted the hospital with the chapel of St Lawrence to Robert Sinclere. In 1477 Edmund Beding-feld granted to John Norris the site of this hospital, which had

[63]

been burnt down, until it would be rebuilt again. There is no evidence however that it was rebuilt.

It was situated on Hardwick Dam at Setchey Parva, in South Lynn.

KING'S LYNN - PILGRIM'S CHAPEL

The chapel was dedicated to Our Lady of the Mount, and was said to have belonged to the 'Guild of Our Lady,' a fraternity founded in Lynn in 1329.

The chapel was completed *c.* 1485 on land forming a mount. The land was granted to the Prior of Lynn by the Corporation.

The building itself is known as the Red Mount and was restored by the Corporation some time ago. It is three stories high with a basement or crypt. It is maintained by the Corporation and can be visited. There is a small fee. It is adjacent to St John's Walk and well worth a visit.

KING'S LYNN - THE BISHOP'S PALACE AT GAYWOOD

The Bishop of Norwich held Gaywood and Lynn in capite, in the time of Henry II (1154-1189).

He would not allow the King's bailiffs or coroners to enter the lordship. Here he had officers of his own, a gallows, assize of bread and beer and other royalties.

Bishop Grey built a palace here. Gaywood Hall was later built on the site. Bishop Grey himself was the fifth Bishop of Norwich from 1200-1221. He was also Lord Chief Justice.

Nothing of the original building remains.

LANGLEY ABBEY, NEAR LODDON.

Premonstratensian Canons

Dedicated to the honour of the Blessed Virgin Mary.

The Abbey was founded by Sir Robert Fitzroger Helke, Lord of Horsford in 1198. He built and endowed the monastery and the grant was confirmed by King John the following

[64]

year. King John himself granted the Abbey several liberties and privileges.

This Abbey was very rich indeed, with many benefactors and the revenues were considerable with property and dues in 80 parishes, with 19 manors, 9 rectories, 4 appropriated churches, with the patronage of two others. Even in 1291 it was valued at £178.5.0¾d.

At the Dissolution it was valued at £104.16.5½d., and granted to John Berney in 1546.

(At the dedication of the Abbey there was an Abbot and 15 canons).

The remains are extensive and are sited adjacent to Abbey Farm, but on private ground. There were over 20 knights buried in the abbey church alone.

LANGWADE LAZAR HOUSE, NEAR STOKE FERRY

The site of this Lazar House was near Langwade Cross. This is sited at the extreme east end of the parish, adjoining that of Cockley Cley.

There was at one time a manor of Langwade, which was situated partly in the decayed parish of Caldecote, which now goes with Oxborough and extended into Cockley Cley.

In 1380 Thomas Salmon, chaplain of Oxborough, gave a legacy to Langwade Lazar House.

LESSINGHAM PRIORY, NEAR STALHAM
Alien, for Benedictine Monks

Dedicated to All Saints.

Sir Thomas de Lessingham is said to be the founder of this alien priory.

The lordship of Lessingham was given by Gerald de Gurney, about the year 1087, to the Abbey of Benedictine monks at Bec in Normandy, which in turn subjected it to their cell at Okeburn in Wiltshire, this being the chief house in England.

This Priory was seized, as it was alien, during the wars with France, by the Parliament of Leicester in 1414. It was dissolved and remained in the care of the Crown for some time. It was then leased to Sir Thomas Erpingham, then to Edmund Clere.

Henry VI (1422-1461) confirmed it by charter to King's College, Cambridge, in 1444. In 1461, Edward IV re-confirmed it to the same college and granted it additional privileges.

In 1291 it was valued at £44.5.0$\frac{1}{4}$d., with property in 8 parishes in Norfolk.

The parish church of All Saints at Lessingham was supposed to have been used by the monks.

The site is said to have been within the churchyard, possibly at the south-east corner. Nothing now remains.

The Master and Fellows of King's College are still in possession of the gift of the living.

LITCHAM PILGRIMS' CHAPEL AND HERMITAGE, NEAR MILEHAM

This Chapel was used by the pilgrims when on their way to the great Shrine at Walsingham. Henry VIII is said to have stopped here. There was also a hermitage attached.

The remains have been turned into a farmhouse. This is north-west of the bridge over the river Nar.

The foundation and the east wall, with double buttresses, are of the original chapel.

LUDHAM BISHOP'S PALACE

The mitred Abbot of St Benet's Abbey had a farm and residence at Ludham, which was afterwards used as a Bishop's Palace. In 1611 it was burnt down.

The Palace is now Ludham Hall and the Bishop's domestic chapel is now a granary. All the remains are on private ground.

LYNG NUNNERY, NEAR EAST DEREHAM   **Benedictine Nuns**

Nothing is known of the foundation or the founder. Most of the nuns were moved to Thetford in 1176, although some lived here in 1249. After this date, a Prior or chaplain was in residence.

In 1438 the Prior of St Edmund's chapel at Lyng was appointed by the Prioress of Thetford Nunnery.

The remains of the chapel are still to be seen at the eastern end of the parish.

MARHAM NUNNERY   **Cistercian Nuns**

The Nunnery was dedicated to the Virgin Mary, St Barbara and St Edmund the King and Confessor.

It was founded in 1249 by Isabella, widow of Hugh de Albany, Earl of Arundel and Sussex. This was the only house of the Cistercian Order in Norfolk.

In 1252 it was made subordinate to the Abbey of Waverley, the principal house in England of Cistercian Nuns. At this time, Henry III confirmed all the grants of the foundress.

It was appropriated with five churches in Norfolk and there were many benefactors, although it was 'considered to have been meanly endowed.' The nunnery was famed for its walnut orchards.

At the Dissolution in 1535, there was an Abbess and eight nuns in residence. It was then valued at £33.13.5d. In 1546 it was sold to Sir Nicholas Hare and John Hare (the latter a citizen of London).

The remains lay a little to the west of the parish church on the opposite side of the road.

MASSINGHAM (GREAT), PRIORY,
NEAR NORTH GRIMSTON   **Augustinian Canons**

The Priory was sometimes called the hospital of St Mary. It was dedicated to the Virgin Mary and St Nicholas.

[67]

It is thought that this priory was founded by Nicholas Le Syre of Massingham about 1260.

In 1291 it was valued at £18.2.0d., with land in six parishes.

In 1475 it consisted of a Prior, two canons and two poor men. At this time the priory was in such a bad state of repair that it was falling down, so it was united to Westacre Priory.

During 1555 the site, with five manors and four advowsons, was granted to Sir Thomas Gresham.

Nothing remains above the foundations. The site is south-west of the village.

MOLYCOURT PRIORY, OUTWELL   Saxon Benedictine Order
Dedicated to St Mary de Bello Loco.

The date and founder are unknown. This was supposed to have been a small Saxon monastery of the Benedictine Order, which was endowed with several lands, rents and services in Norfolk and Suffolk. However, in 1445, it could only support one monk as it was so poor, so at this time Henry VI licensed the prior to place himself under the protection of the priory of Ely, and in 1449 Walter Lyhart, the Bishop of Norwich, appropriated it to Ely monastery.

In 1291 it was valued at £9.2.8d. At the most, the priory consisted of a Prior and two or three monks.

It is interesting to note that it was so poor in 1385, that the Bishop of Ely would grant forty days' pardon to all who would become benefactors.

At the Dissolution it was valued with Ely.

There are no remains above the foundations. It is sited on the east side of the main road from Wisbech to Downham Market, just over a mile south-east of the parish church.

The site is now partly occupied by a farmhouse.

[68]

NORMANSBURGH PRIORY, SOUTH RAYNHAM

Cluniac Monks

Dedicated to the Blessed Virgin Mary and St John the Evangelist.

This small Priory was founded by William de Lisewise in 1160, for, as it was said, the health of his own soul and those of his wife Maud and Godfrey his son.

His son Godfrey later gave it to the monastery of Castleacre on the condition that they kept here at least three Cluniac monks.

It was endowed with several lands, including a Hermitage at Wiggenhall St Mary Magdalen, a lordship and St Martin's church at South Raynham, plus various rents and services.

In 1291 it was valued at £6.0.10d. At the Dissolution it was valued with Castleacre.

In 1538 it was granted to Thomas, Duke of Norfolk. It then went to Roger Townsend in 1564. It still remains with the Townshend family who live at South Raynham.

Nothing remains above the foundations.

The site is at Normansburgh, which is in the eastern part of the parish of South Raynham, or Raynham St Martin, as it is called.

NORTON SUBCOURSE COLLEGE, NEAR LODDON

Secular Canons

Originally Raveningham College.

Dedicated to the Virgin Mary.

The original College was at Raveningham and was founded about 1350 by Sir John de Norwich and his wife Margaret. Sir John was Vice Admiral of England.

It was for secular canons who also officiated in the church at Raveningham, and they were to pray for the souls of the founder and his wife. At this time there was a Master and eight secular canons.

[69]

The college was well endowed by the founder with 8 manors, the advowsons and appropriations of Raveningham church, and many lands and tenements in 12 parishes.

In 1387 the college was removed to Norton Subcourse, the adjoining parish, by licence from Richard II. The college was established in the Rectory house there. A new chapel was built and the number of canons was augmented to twelve, plus the Master.

The advowsons of St Margaret's church at Norton Subcourse had been given to the College by the founder in 1350. His grandson, Sir John de Norwich, gave £450 in 1373 towards the building of a new church.

In 1393 the college was moved again by licence from Richard II to the Castle of Mettingham in Suffolk.

The college, with the appropriated rectories of Norton Subcourse and Raveningham, and the Castle of Mettingham in Suffolk, were granted to Sir Anthony Denny in 1541.

Nothing remains above the foundations. The site at Raveningham is surrounded by a moat.

NORWICH

Norwich in the Middle Ages was the second or third city in England. Before the Dissolution there were at least thirty monastic institutions, several of which have now entirely disappeared, although the sites are known. Some of these were quite small hospitals or almshouses, but they all came under the care of monks and nuns and were part of the great monastic system.

At the present time, Norwich still possesses thirty-two, still-standing medieval churches, but at least another twenty-nine have completely gone to decay.

At one time the City was surrounded by a wall, except where it was protected by the River Wensum, that is, from Carrow Bridge to the Cow Tower. This wall was started in 1294 and finished in 1309. Although much time and money had been spent on it, the walls were falling down and much decayed even before it was supposedly finished, so yet more time and money was spent and it was finally completed in 1319 or 1320. By this time it had forty towers and twelve gates.

A fair amount is preserved, the best stretch being at Carrow Hill. The wall can be followed from near Carrow Bridge, along Carrow Hill and Bracondale. It turns at Ber Street and follows the line of Queens Road and Chapelfield Road, along Chapelfield Gardens. The wall goes down the hill just east of Grapes Hill and appears again south of Bakers Road and Magpie Road. At Magdalen Gate there is a better preserved piece ending inside the public lavatory.

There is a polygonal tower in Wall Lane, just north of Barrack Street and the wall finishes at Cow Tower. This is the best tower, being 50 feet high and 36 feet across and built of brick. The stretch from Cow Tower to Carrow Bridge is protected by the river.

The walls were about 20 feet high and the towers were semi-circular, with one or two being semi-polygonal.

Most of the monastic institutions were within the walls, except for St Leonard's Priory and the Chapel of St Michael on the Mount, these were on the hill opposite Bishopsgate Bridge. St Catherine's Priory was on Mousehold Heath, and the Priory of Benedictine nuns was sited to the left of Bracondale going down the hill, just before the bridge.

Most of the leper houses were sited just outside the City gates.

Norwich City Central Library possesses much information on the monastic establishments in the City.

NORWICH CATHEDRAL   **Benedictine Priory**

The East Angles were converted to the Christian faith by Felix, a Burgundian who became the first Bishop of his new

[71]

converts and placed his See at Dunwich, around the year 630 AD.

In 673 the fourth Bishop divided the diocese, continuing with one Bishop at Dunwich, who had the jurisdiction over the county of Suffolk, and placing another at North Elmham, whose pastoral care was confined to that of Norfolk.

About 870, the Sees were united and the place of the Bishop's residence fixed at Elmham.

In 1075, in consequence of a decree of the council held by Lanfranc, Archbishop of Canterbury, the See was removed to Thetford, where it continued until 1094, when Herbert de Losinga finally fixed it at Norwich.

The first stone was laid by Bishop Herbert in 1096, followed by the laying of stones by the nobles and barons of the diocese, including Roger Bigod, Earl of Norfolk, and Baron de Rye, both contributing towards the endowments.

By 1100 the work had progressed so well that Bishop Herbert obtained a licence from the Archbishop of Canterbury to instal monks instead of secular canons.

Sixty monks settled here under the government of a Prior who was to be elected by the majority of them.

The list of benefactors is one of the longest of any monastic establishment in East Anglia. At the time of the Norwich Taxation in 1291, the value was given at £932.18.6½d., with revenues in 152 parishes. At the Dissolution in 1538, William Castleton, then the Prior, surrendered the monastery into the hands of the King, who, on May 2nd of the same year, granted the new foundation for a dean, six prebendaries and six choral vicars or minor canons and appointed the said William Castleton as dean.

In 1547 it was re-founded and incorporated by the name of 'The Dean and Chapter of the Cathedral Church of the Holy and Undivided Trinity of Norwich, of the Foundation of King Edward VI.'

It then consisted of one dean, six prebendaries, six petty canons, one gospeller, one epestler, one organist, eight lay clerks, eight choristers, six poor men maintained out of the revenues of the church, two vergers, two sub-sacrists, one high steward, one under steward of courts, one chapter clerk, etc.

Subordinate to the Cathedral Priory and all founded or endowed by Bishop Herbert de Losinga, were the cells or priories of St Leonard's on Mousehold, King's Lynn, Yarmouth, North Elmham, Aldeby and Hoxne in Suffolk.

The history of the Cathedral Priory is very varied and chequered. The prior and monks were continually on bad terms with the citizens of Norwich as can be seen from some of the following extracts.

In 1171 the church was considerably damaged by fire, which seems to have been accidental. This was repaired by John of Oxford, the fourth Bishop, about the year 1197. He completely refitted and ornamented the church and presented it with a new set of vestments.

During 1263 several citizens of Norwich were prosecuted for setting fire to each others' houses. At this time the city was divided into two groups. The bishop and clergy, with the barons, who were in arms against the King, while the city bailiffs and commons declared for the royal party. These two divisions revived old grudges between the citizens and the monks and many lives were lost.

On 29th June, 1271, the cathedral steeple was violently struck by lightning. Several large stones were thrown down with great force and the choir was filled with stench and smoke. This happened when the monks were at prime.

In 1272, at a fair granted to the church by charter on Trinity Sunday (Easter Sunday) at Tombland in front of the monastery gates, there arose a quarrel between the citizens and the servants of the monastery. It seems that some of the citizens were killed. Warrants were issued for the arrest of the murderers wherever they could be found.

[73]

This warrant highly provoked the monks. They insisted that the place where the dispute arose was in their jurisdiction and entirely exempt from that of the city magistrates.

The monks then procured a number of hired men, who shut up the gates and fired upon the citizens as they passed by. Several were wounded.

On the Sunday before St Lawrence's Day, the hired men sallied forth into the city, which they ravaged all day and night, killing several merchants and plundering their houses.

The king was informed, and the magistrates ordered the citizens to meet the next day on the market place at ten in the morning.

The citizens then attacked the monastery from every side. They set fire to the great gates and the nearby church of St Albert's.

The whole of the Cathedral church was fired except for the Virgin Mary's Chapel, together with the dormitory, refectory, entertaining hall and the infirmary, the chapel belonging to the infirmary and the majority of buildings in the court.

Many of the sub-deacons, clerks and laymen were killed in the cloisters and precincts of the monastery. Others were carried out and killed in the city. Some were imprisoned.

The whole monastery was then plundered of gold, silver, holy vessels, books and vestments.

Most of the monks had fled by this time, leaving behind two or three very aged ones. When all this damage had been wrought on the monastery, the citizens turned on the favourers of the church and plundered their houses.

The Prior, William de Brunham, fled to Yarmouth, hired a company of armed men, came back to Norwich and entered the city sword in hand and in his turn fell to killing the citizens and destroying their houses.

The King came to Norwich to punish the people on September 14th. Such were the times when punishment was harsh, for thirty-four of the offenders were drawn by horses through the streets until they died. Others were hanged and quartered and their bodies afterwards burnt. The woman who set fire to the gates was slowly burnt alive. The city was fined 3,000 marks towards the rebuilding of the church. The city also had to pay out £100 for a cup weighing ten pounds in gold for the monastery.

The Prior, who was in great measure the cause of things coming to this extremity, was committed to the Bishop's Priory. He resigned the Priory into the Bishop's hands on 28th September and William de Kirkely was elected Prior in his place.

On 15th January, 1361, the steeple of the Cathedral was blown down and fell into the choir. Bishop Percy gave £400 towards its rebuilding and obtained an aid of 9d. in the pound from his clergy for the same purpose.

1452. During this year the bad feeling between the Prior and the city broke out afresh, but was at length settled by the Bishop of Norwich.

1463. On the 1st March of this year the Cathedral was considerably damaged again by fire, and the Cathedral church was damaged by lightning.

1486. Trouble again between the Prior and the citizens, with respect to their liberties.

The Prior insisted that the site of the Priory, Holmstrete, Tombland, Raton Row, etc., were not in the jurisdiction of the City. This dispute lasted many years and cost both parties a lot of money.

1507. During this year the Bishop of Norwich, Richard Rix, condemned Thomas Norris for the true profession of the gospel. He was burnt alive.

1430. The cloister was finished in this year, one hundred and thirty-three years from its first being undertaken.

It is interesting to note the tomb of Bishop Anthony de Beck. He was clerk in the court of Rome and was made Bishop by the Pope's mandate. He was a restless person and much

[75]

hated. He was poisoned by his own servant and died 19th December, 1343.

Near this tomb is buried Thomas Percy, brother to the Earl of Northumberland. He was made Bishop when he was 21 years of age by the authority of the Pope and at the request of Henry, Duke of Lancaster. He was elected against the will of the monks who could not be persuaded to choose him. He died at Blofield on 8th August, 1369.

Walter de Suffield, the tenth Bishop, from 1244-1257, built the chapel of the Virgin Mary, also called St Mary the Great.

He was a much-loved Bishop and very revered for his sanctity and goodness. His shrine was visited by pilgrims from various parts and numerous miracles were said to be wrought at his tomb.

This chapel of St Mary's escaped during the insurrection in 1272 by the citizens, when most of the adjoining buildings were defaced by fire.

Before the Reformation, there was a small chapel called the Holy-rood chapel (rode, Saxon for Cross). This place was a repository for holy relics, amongst which was yet another portion of the blood of the Blessed Virgin Mary, to which many came in pilgrimage and made their offerings. Once a week, Jesus's Mass was sung here.

There was a representation here of the Holy Trinity. In 1499, Margaret, wife of the late Sir Ralph Shelton, presented this image with a large golden chain weighing nearly eight ounces, with one large jewel with a red rose enamelled in gold hanging thereto, and four smaller jewels. Before this, in 1443, Robert Norwich gave to this same image a silver collar given to him by the Emperor.

The magnificent Cathedral and cloisters still remain. The monastic buildings are nearly all destroyed, but the sites are marked by small tablets. The four gateways of the precincts still remain, the Water Gate, Bishop's Palace Gates, the Erpingham Gate and the Ethelbert Gate.

[76]

The Charnel House chapel and crypt are preserved and are part of the King Edward VI School.

NORWICH - ST CATHERINE'S CHAPEL AND PRIORY
Benedictine Monks

This Chapel and Priory was originally dedicated to St Catherine, then in the middle of the 12th century it was re-consecrated to St William of Norwich.

It was at first a parochial church, founded about the time of the Conquest. Some time after it was re-consecrated to the honour of St William at Norwich, the boy who was supposedly crucified by the Jews at Thorpe. The chapel was then called St William in the Wood.

Adjoining this chapel was a cell or priory of Benedictine monks from Norwich Cathedral. They were maintained out of the profits of the churches of Lakenham and Arminghall.

In 1230, Nigel de Hapesburgh founded a chantry here for his own and his ancestor's souls and enlarged the revenues.

During 1256 it was appropriated to the office of almoner of the convent, and about 1410 united to the parish of St James.

At the Dissolution it was completely demolished, the site was then known as Pockthorpe churchyard. It was granted to the Dean and Chapter of Norwich. Up to the Dissolution it was used a lot by pilgrims.

In 1550 it was leased by the Dean and Chapter to William Blenerhaysett, by the name of, the chapel yard called St William in the Wood.

The site is 200 to 300 yards due west of the junction of Gurney Road and Mousehold Lane. The foundations can be traced of the church and monastic buildings. The boundary of the precinct is marked at the four corners by stone posts. Two of these posts can be seen from the ring road opposite the war memorial cottages.

On Advent Sunday, 1278, the Bishop of London dedicated the altar where the body of St William was buried, to the honour of Our Saviour and All Saints.

NORWICH - ST LEONARD'S PRIORY   Benedictine Monks

Dedicated to the Honour of God and St Leonard.

The monastery was built and founded by Herbert de Losinga before he built the cathedral priory. It was a cell to the cathedral until the Dissolution. It was governed by a Prior, appointed by the Prior of Norwich and confirmed by the Bishop.

The monks from this priory performed daily service in the adjacent chapel of St Michael on the Mount, of which the ruins remain but on private land. This was founded around 1100.

St Leonard's church was famed because of its image of Henry III, which was visited by pilgrims from all parts, for the cure of their diseases of whatever kind they were.

The monks were supplied from the cathedral priory and generally contained a Prior and seven or eight monks.

At the Dissolution it was valued with Norwich and the property went to the Crown.

The priory was granted, in 1538, to Thomas, Duke of Norfolk, whose son, Henry Howard, Earl of Surrey, built on its site a sumptuous house which he called Surrey House, as the hill on which it was built is called Mount Surrey.

The Earl was beheaded and the property went to the Crown again. Queen Elizabeth, in 1562, granted it to Thomas, Duke of Norfolk and his heirs.

The priory was totally demolished by Kett during his rebellion. The site contained about 14 acres.

The site and remains are situated at the corner of Gas Hill and St Leonard's Road. There are lengths of walls and foundations left, all are on private ground. There is a well which is 160 feet deep and supposedly of Roman origin. This is south-west of the site. St Michael's chapel stands a few hundred yards to the north.

The priory is on a hill overlooking the river Wensum. Under the priory the followers of John Wycliffe, one of the first Reformers, were burnt for Lollardy. Since then the place has been known as Lollard's Pit.

NORWICH - PRIORY OF BLACK FRIARS, 1st HOUSE
Dominican Friars

Dedicated to St John the Baptist.

The first friars of this Order came to Norwich in 1226, and seated themselves in the church of St John the Baptist, then parochial and a rectory.

They then procured this church to be made conventual, with the parish united to St George in Colgate.

This first house was sited between the churches of St George at Colegate, and St Clement's, both remain, and St Mary Unburnt, which stood at the corner of Golden Dog Lane.

They were settled here by Sir Thomas Gelham, who gave them the church and a house to live in. Henry III confirmed the grant and gave a gift of ten marks himself.

The church of St John the Baptist, now destroyed, stood slightly west of where the Octogon Chapel now stands.

In 1261 William de Dunwich and his wife Catherine gave to the Friars a garden on the west side of their site. In 1273 Sir Richard de Norwich gave them a yard and messuage, opposite the previous gift, extending from the street to the river, and in 1281 they enclosed their site with a wall.

The Prioress of Carrow gave the friars a messuage in 1290. Also during this year, Roger de Penteneye gave them a gift of land.

In 1299 two clerks, John de Acle and Thomas de Depham, each gave a messuage. Several local clergy and merchants also gave gifts and grants.

The Prior and Brethren moved in 1308 to the site where St Andrew's Hall now stands. After they left, the old site was called Blackhall.

They continued to perform services in the church or chapel and a hermit was placed there to look after it.

At the Dissolution the old site was granted to the Corporation. In time, all the buildings were destroyed.

PRIORY OF BLACK FRIARS, 2nd HOUSE   Dominican Friars

The second house was also dedicated to St John the Baptist.

The site was first occupied by the Friars de Sacco, or Brethren of the Sac. They were suppressed in 1307.

Edward I licensed the Black Friars to settle in a new site in the parishes of St Peter Hungate and St Andrew's. He reserved to the last Prior of the Brethren of the Sac, then living but decrepit with age, his dwelling and maintenance during life.

Petronel de Nerford, a widow, and daughter of Sir John de Vallibus, released all her rights in the new site, which was formerly her father's inheritance and by him given to the Brethren of the Sac.

Her sister Maud, wife of Sir William de Roos of Hamlok, also released her rights.

In 1310 William Butt and Christian his wife, with the licence of Edward II, gave the friars a piece of land 500 feet long and 400 feet broad, with a quay lying at Newbrigge.

From then on the list of benefactors is considerable, including many from nobility.

The site, after gifts of land, when completed extended from St Andrew's Street on the south side of the river to Golden Dog Lane on the north. Where the Friars of the Sac had their church, the Black Friars built the choir of their new church. This is now called Blackfriars Hall.

The nave of the conventual church, now called St Andrew's Hall, was built at the expense of Sir Thomas Erpingham who died in 1428 before it was finished. It was completed by his

[80]

son, Sir Robert Erpingham, who was rector of Bracon Ash, and a friar of this priory.

There were five altars in the conventual church and four side chapels. Nine images were placed inside the church, including one of the Holy Rood and one of Our Lady.

As already stated, the Friars moved to this site in 1308, but in 1413 the house, church, etc., were entirely destroyed by fire. This obliged them to return to their old situation on the other side of the river. They lived here till a second fire in 1499 forced them back again before their church and buildings was completed.

The new monastery was then finished in 1485 and Richard III confirmed all the rights and privileges that had been given and the Pope did the same.

In 1331 it seems as if the City Fathers were getting worried at the way the new monastery was growing.

'In 1331, the city being displeased at their getting into their possession and demolishing so many houses, prevailed upon the excheator to seize all such as had been given or purchased without licence in mortmain. But notwithstanding this, in 1351 they were all with several others, lately given, confirmed to them by the King.'

At the Dissolution, the City, through the interest of the Duke of Norfolk in 1540, obtained a grant of the convent, and all that belonged to it, 'to make of the church (according to the petition) a fair and large hall, for the mayor and his brethren, with all the citizens, to repair unto at common assemblies, and to have a pulpit for all strangers, and others, to preach in every Sunday and holiday in the forenoon and afternoon, when there was no services at the Cathedral cross, and to make a chapel of the choir for the citizens' priest to perform daily service in and also at their assemblies and to make of the dorter and frater, granaries to lay up the City's store of corn for the poor, and to maintain the malt house, mill-house and bake house, for the City's profit, and to let out

[81]

the site, orchards, etc., and to maintain the church and the houses belonging to it.'

The cloister and conventual buildings were all on the north side of the church and extended to the river. The cloister garth is still open with the south walk still intact. The other sides have been built on.

St Andrew's Hall, next to the cloisters, is still used by the Corporation. Part of the site is occupied by the Art School. The cloister is to be renovated shortly with a new chapel and entrance into Elm Hill. This might prove interesting as several clergy and nobility were supposed to have been buried within the cloister garth.

The actual number of monks at this monastery is unknown.

NORWICH - PRIORY OF GREY FRIARS   **Franciscan Friars**
Dedicated to St Francis.

The Franciscans, or Friar Minors, first came to Norwich in 1226. They settled in a house given to them by John de Hastingford, situated in Conisford, between the churches of St Vedast and St Cuthbert.

In 1284 they obtained a licence from Edward I to enclose and take into their site a common lane, and in 1288 procured a confirmation of their foundation and the liberty of making purchases to enlarge the precincts. This they were well able to do from the large and numerous benefactions they had received. Soon after this the church was started and was a very large building : 'From the west window to the folding doors at the tower or steeple was a 150 feet, from thence to the folding doors entering the choir being the interspace for the belfry or steeple, 50 feet, the breadth of the nave and aisles were about 80 feet, the length 150 feet nearly, and the breadth 50 feet. The cloister on the south side was a quadrangle, its side equal to the length of the nave. The church was finished in the space of a few years and dedicated to St Francis.'

It also possessed a fine chapter house on the east side of the cloister, being about 130 feet long. This was sometimes used for public business. It also possesed a very fine library, but this was destroyed at the Dissolution.

In the church were several images and two chapels to Our Saviour and St Anne.

One of the cloisters of the monastery was called the 'Pardon Cloister' because of the indulgences granted by the Pope to all such persons as should be buried there. This brought in much revenue to the monks.

During 1537 the Lord Surrey lodged here, and soon after the monastery was dissolved and the site and church granted to Thomas, Duke of Norfolk. In 1544 it was seized by the King and granted in part to Paul Gresham and Francis Boldeio. The part of the site not vested, reverted to the Norfolk family on Queen Mary's reversing the attainder.

The Duke sold it to the Corporation in 1559 for £200.

The site was in the vicinity of Prince of Wales Road and Greyfriars Road. It is now occupied by the premises of Mann Egerton & Co., Ltd.

Everything is completely destroyed of the church and monastic buildings.

At one time two anchoretages adjoined the precincts.

NORWICH - PRIORY OF WHITE FRIARS   Carmelite Friars

The Priory was dedicated to the Holy and Blessed Virgin Mary.

Its founder was Philip Ernold or Arnold, also called Philip de Cowgate as he resided in Cowgate. He settled his messuage and lands in Cowgate on William de Suffield, Archdeacon of Norwich, and his heirs, on condition that the Brethren of Mount Carmel should take possession of and dwell there, without any molestation whatever.

These friars, through the benevolence of their founder and other benefactors, soon erected a noble church here, and when

[83]

it was finished the founder himself took the Order and habit of a Carmelite and entered the house. He died on 23rd April, 1283, and was buried in the church.

At his death, at the request of the Prior and convent, the patronage of their house was accepted by the mayor, aldermen, sheriffs and citizens of Norwich, and this their acceptance confirmed in the general chapter of their Order held at Burnham.

This house had many benefactions, but these consisted mainly of money and goods. It was contrary to their rules to have any possessions except for the site of their houses in which they dwelt, although this rule was sometimes broken under the the pretence of conveniency.

In 1400 the Archbishop of Canterbury, Thomas Arundel, was received and entertained here.

In 1498 the Prior and brethren were exempted from the payment of any toll and custom in the City, as well as from all fees due to the city officers, for everything used and consumed in their house.

In the conventual church there were two chapels, of St Mary and of the Holy Cross. There was also the Guild of St Barbara and the images of St Anne, Our Lady and St Laurence.

Many important people were buried in the priory church, most of them being benefactors to the monastery.

To the monastery belonged two houses for anchorets. One was near St Martin's bridge on the east side of the river with a small garden reaching down to the river. This was inhabited by a brother.

The other was under the chapel of the Holy Cross, inhabited by a sister.

The monastery was suppressed in 1543 and granted to Robert Andrews and Leonard Chamberlain, by letters patent, dated 17th June, to hold to them and their heirs, of the king in capite by Knights service. The property was soon divided up.

The site is to the east of Cowgate and immediately to the south of St James' parish church.

Nothing remains of the original buildings of the monastery. The church of the priory stood near that of St James, at one time only a passage divided the two churchyards.

NORWICH - PRIORY OF WHITE FRIARS,
ST MARTIN'S PRIORY   Carmelite Friars

At St Martin's in the Bailey was a small Priory. The founder and date of foundation is unknown.

It is known that a fraternity of friars lived in a house situated in the churchyard until they were obliged to join one of the four principal Orders, when they united themselves to the White Friars or Carmelites.

The Church was often called St Martin at the Castle Gate, or St Martin's Priory.

It was of ancient foundation and originally belonged to the castle. It was given by William the Conqueror to Ralph Fitz-Walter. At one time all persons dying in the castle were buried here. On the south side of the churchyard stood a cross called St Martin's Cross.

The church was completely demolished in 1565. Nothing remains.

The site was south of the castle near Golden Ball Street and Rising Sun Lane.

NORWICH - PRIORY OF AUSTIN FRIARS   Augustinian Friars

Dedicated to St Mary the Virgin and St Augustine.

The Austin Friars came to this City in the beginning of the reign of Edward I, and settled themselves in a messuage given them by Roger Minniot who, on this account, was esteemed their founder.

Their first charter of foundation is dated 1293, and in 1319 they procured another to confirm their possessions.

[85]

In 1360 they possessed the whole of St Michael's parish on the east side of the street, except for the church and churchyard. This they soon purchased and pulled down.

On the site of this church and of their former dwelling house they built a cloister and conventual church, 150 yards long and 30 yards wide, with a second cloister on its south side. The whole site was enclosed by a high wall and was finished in 1368.

In 1429 they obtained a charter of confirmation of their foundation and revenues.

The Friars of this monastery possessed many privileges, being exempt from the Bishop's jurisdiction and from being immediately subject to the Pope.

The many benefactors included several prominent people. Sir Thomas Erpingham, who was a great benefactor to the Black Friars, was also a patron of the Austin Friars. In the monastery church there were three Guilds, St Augustine or the Shoemaker's Guild, of the Holy Cross and of St Margaret's.

The greatest profit to the convent was the Chapel of Our Lady called Scala Coeli, to which the pilgrims flocked and made their offerings on the altar there. This was because of the many pardons and indulgences granted by the Pope to this place.

At the Dissolution the monastery went to Henry VIII, and at his death it went to his son, Edward VI. In 1547 he granted it to Sir Thomas Heneage and Catherine his wife, and William, Lord Willoughby. It was later sold to Sir John Godsalve.

At this monastery at Conisford Place were orchards and gardens and fishing.

Part of the site is occupied by Watney Mann's brewery at Conisford.

All that remains is a few old walls.

[86]

NORWICH - PRIORY OF THE FRIARS DE SACCO

Also called *De Penitentia Jusu* and *Brethren of the Sac*.

Dedicated to the Virgin Mary.

These friars settled here in Norwich around 1250, in a house opposite St Peter Hungate church, and in the yard belonging to the house built an oratory or church, dedicated to the Virgin Mary.

In 1258 John de Vaux gave them a messuage in St Andrew's parish joining the west part of their house.

In 1271 their foundation was confirmed by Simon, rector of St Peter of Hungate, and the Dean and Chapter of the college of St Mary's in the Field, patrons of St Peter's.

They obtained a licence to appropriate the yard and houses given to them by their founder to their own use, on finding four people who were willing to enter into an engagement to save the rector of St Peter's any loss to the profits of his living.

On this condition, they were permitted to have an oratory or private chapel in their house and a church and steeple, with liberty to celebrate all divine services therein, ring their bells and bury their dead.

This agreement was confirmed by Roger, 12th Bishop of Norwich.

Shortly after, Robert Laddings, a shoe-maker and his wife Amy, gave them a messuage in St Andrew's, and in 1276 William Butt confirmed to them a piece of land in St Andrew's adjoining their site.

The Order was suppressed in 1307 and the convent was granted to the Black Friars.

William de Hoe, the last Prior of the Brethren of the Sac, was granted his dwelling and maintenance for life. At this time he was still living but very old.

The site of this old Order is now occupied by Blackfriars Hall.

NORWICH - PRIORY OF FRIARS OF OUR LADY
Fratres de Domina

On the south side of St Julian's churchyard stood a house of Friars of the Order of Our Lady, called *Fratres de Domina,* a kind of begging friars, who observed the Rule of St Augustine.

They wore a white coat, over which was a black cloak and a black cowl.

The Order was introduced into Norwich in 1290. Roger de Tybenham gave them a legacy soon after their establishment. They continued here until the reign of Edward III, when all the brethren died of the plague in 1348. Their house then became private property.

No buildings remain, except for a part of old wall.

According to the 'History of Norfolk,' printed 1778-1789, on the east side of the churchyard stood an anchorage, inhabited by an anchoress or recluse, until the Dissolution.

In the 1370's Lady Julian resided here. She is known as one of the most famous English mystics. She did not, however, live on the east side of the Church, but in a cell adjoining the south side of the church.

The church of St Julian was bombed during the war. It has now been completely rebuilt. The foundations of St Julian's cell can still be traced.

Near this church, in 1296, the Lady Cecily de Howe, the Prioress of Carrow, had a house built for the prioresses to reside in whenever they pleased.

This residence later came into the possession of the Bardolfs and was known as Bardolf's Place.

NORWICH - PRIORY OR FRATERNITY OF FRIARS OF THE BLESSED MARY, ST NICHOLAS AND ALL SAINTS

These Friars lived in a house situated in the churchyard of

St Martin's in the Bailey, until they were obliged to unite themselves to the Carmelites in 1307.

See Norwich – Priory of Carmelite Friars. (St Martin's Priory).

NORWICH - PRIORY OF PIED FRIARS

These Friars were called Pied Friars, from their garments, which were black and white like a magpie. Their house was at the north-east corner of the churchyard of St Peter Permountergate.

The Order was suppressed in 1307 and the brethren were obliged to join one of the four principal Orders. When the friars left their house it was dissolved to the hospital at Bec in Billingsford. The house became a college of priests.

NORWICH - COLLEGE OF SECULAR CANONS

The College was dedicated to the Holy Trinity.

When the Pied Friars quitted their residence at the north-east corner of St Peter's churchyard, it was turned into a College of Secular Canons, subordinate to the hospital at Bec in Billingsford.

The Master of this hospital used the College at St Peter's as his city headquarters. Here, he received 'All such chauntry or soul priests, or secular canons, as had served in this church, or anywhere else. Here they lived quite in a collegiate manner, paying for their commons and continued to do so till the Dissolution.'

In the church of St Peter's at Permountergate can be seen the ancient stalls used by the canons or, as they were called then, chauntry and soul priests. There are 24 stalls.

Nothing remains of the college.

Incidentally, Thomas Codd, a city magistrate, lies buried here in the middle aisle. He was Mayor of the city during Kett's Rebellion in 1549. He was a benefactor to this church, it appears that 'Thomas Codd esquire, gave £10 per annum to the curate, to the poor 10/- per annum, and four nobles for Knight's meat.' Citizens or knights meat being the daily allowance to the burgesses or knights of shires, during their attendance in Parliament, paid to them by their constituents.

NORWICH - COLLEGE OF ST MARY IN THE FIELDS
Prebendaries and Chantry

This College was dedicated to the Blessed Virgin Mary.

Originally it was called the Chapel in the Fields, it being at its foundation a chapel of the Blessed Virgin Mary.

It was founded before 1250, by a priest called John le Brun of Norwich, and was at that time a hospital. The benefactors and grants to the hospital were so great that in a short time it became a college, consisting of a Dean, Chancellor, precentor, treasurer and seven prebendaries. Eight chaplains or chantry priests were afterwards added to the foundation.

There were also several guild chaplains and soul priests, who shared a common table and lived in a collegiate manner. The founder was the first Dean.

The Dean was collated by the Bishop in right of the See, or by the King during a vacancy.

The benefactors were many, including bishops and several titled persons.

In 1291 it was valued at £4.10.3d., with property in 21 parishes, and in 1534 it was valued at £86.12.8d.

Just before the Dissolution the College was endowed with the patronage and advowsons of 11 churches, with the manors of Bowthorpe and Easton, and possessions in about 29 parishes in Norfolk.

There are many documents and old wills relating to this college and most of the history of benefactors and grants are known, but the list is too long to mention here.

Eight chantries were founded in this College between 1331 and 1497. One of these was founded by William Sedman, citizen of Norwich in 1411. He settled on the College the manor and advowson of Bowthorpe with one messuage, one toft, 320 acres of arable and pasture land, six acres of meadow, 16 acres of marsh, seven acres of broom and annual rents to the amount of nine shillings.

At the Dissolution, Miles Spencer, LLD, the last Dean, persuaded the college to resign their revenues for a very small pension, after he had obtained a grant of the whole college for himself and heirs, from Henry VIII. The College was dissolved in 1545.

The site was where the Assembly Rooms at Theatre Street now stands. There are small fragments of the original building in the west wall.

Under the building, however, are old vaults and crypts, all belonging to the medieval College.

NORWICH - HOSPITAL OF ST GILES AT BISHOPSGATE

Dedicated to the Honour of God, the Virgin Mary, St Anne, St Giles and All Saints.

The Hospital was founded in 1249 by Walter Suffield, alias Calthorpe, Bishop of Norwich.

The original church of St Helen which belonged to the monks of the Cathedral was pulled down in 1249-1250, when the present hospital and church were built on the opposite side of the street and dedicated to St Giles.

The foundation deed, executed by Bishop Suffield, is dated at Norwich, October, 1249, 'by which he gave and confirmed to God, the Virgin Mary, St Anne and All Saints, and to the hospital of his foundation at Norwich, to their honour, all those messuages which he purchased in Norwich, of Henry de Salle, Robert de Stanford, for the use of the Master and brethren of the hospital, together with the churches of Calthorpe, Costesy, Cringleford and South Walsham St Mary, all which he appropriated to the hospital with the consent of the Prior and Chapter, for the maintenance of four chaplains to

[91]

celebrate daily service for his soul forever, all the poor and decrepit chaplains in the diocese of Norwich who had not wherewith to maintain themselves, and thirteen other poor people who were to be lodged in the house, and to have one meal a day.'

William de Donewyco, or Dunwich, burgess of Norwich, gave a meadow near Bishop's Bridge extending from the river to the hospital, and 6/8d. rent in Holme Street, to find 13 pints of wine yearly for the Prior, plus, amongst other gifts, a considerable amount of money to provide for five sick people in the hospital. For this he was commemorated as a co-founder of the hospital.

After this there were many benefactors so that previous to the Dissolution the hospital held the impropriation of 11 churches with six manors and rents, with services and rents in upwards of thirty parishes in Norfolk.

In the collegiate church were chapels and oratories and the altars of St Catherine and St Nicholas.

It seems that in 1310 the hospital was prospering well, as the four chantry chaplains were added to, so that there were eight brethren, who all wore the habit of regular canons.

In 1430 the hospital consisted of 'A Master, eight chaplains, two clerks, seven poor scholars choristers, eight poor people who lodged there, and thirteen others who daily dined there, with two sisters to attend the poor in the hospital, with as many poor travellers as the beds set apart for that purpose would hold, were entertained for one night, plus the poor chaplain of the diocese worn out with age or labouring under such infirmities as disabling them from officiating, were wholly maintained.'

By the return in 1534, it appeares that alms were annually distributed to 180 poor people on the Feast of the Annunciation.

The Master and brethren subscribed to the King's supremacy in 1534, and in 1547 the patron, master and brethren surrendered the hospital to Edward VI.

Edward VI granted the dissolved hospital to the City of Norwich for the relief of poor people to be called God's House, and to be united with the parish of St Helen.

In 1534 the value was given at £90.12.0d., by 1549 it had risen to £142.19.2½d.

The Great Hospital at Bishopsgate, as it is now called, is still used. It is maintained and governed by Trustees as an old people's home.

The original plan can still be made out in spite of additions and changes. Much remains, including the church. The building was over 200 feet long. To the north of the infirmary hall lies a cloister. The church is open to the public. The majority of the parish belongs to this hospital.

NORWICH - GOD'S HOUSE IN ST GILES

Hospital and Poor House

During the reign of Edward I (1272-1307) John le Grant gave an almshouse in Lower Newport to the parish. The gift was confirmed in 1310 by Thomas le Grant, his son. Some time before 1472 it was rebuilt by Bishop Walter Lyhart.

Just before the Dissolution the poor people here were nominated by the Bishop. In 1534 it was seized with the other revenues of the See.

The site was on the north side of Lower St Giles Street, mid-way between Willow Lane and Fishers Lane. There are no remains.

Over St Giles Gates lived a hermit.

In the churchyard of St Giles was a hermitage.

NORWICH - GOD'S HOUSE IN ST MARGARET'S   Poor House

This was an almshouse for the poor, called God's House in St Margaret's. It was given by Robert de Ashwardby in 1292.

[93]

It was sited on the north side of St Benedict's Street, on the west side of St Margaret's Street.

There are no remains.

NORWICH - ST MARGARET'S ALMSHOUSE   Poor House

The house was founded in 1463. It was sited at the north-east corner of St Margaret's churchyard. There is very little known about it other than its existence.

There are no remains.

NORWICH - HILDEBROND'S HOSPITAL

Also called Hildebrond's Spital, Ivy Hall or St Mary's Hospital.

It was dedicated to the Honour of the Blessed Virgin Mary and the hospital chapel was dedicated to Edward the Confessor.

The hospital was founded about 1216 by Hildebrond the Mercer and Maud his wife, they gave the patronage to the Bishop. The land was purchased by the founder from Roger de Dunewig.

It consisted of a common hall with a large chamber over it for the use of the custos or keeper, and several smaller rooms, both up and down, for the use as lodgings for such poor people as wanted habitation. Besides the lodging, a fire was allowed them.

The chapel for the service of the hospital was joined to the west end of St Edward's church. St Edward's stood to the south-west of St Julian's church.

In 1269 the parish of St Edward was united with the parish of St Julian. After this St Edward's church became entirely appropriated to the hospital. The rector was discharged from the service of St Edward's and the chapel was only occasionally used by the hospital chaplain.

The hospital was used mainly for the reception of poor, homeless people, in charge was a Master and several brethren.

[94]

The mastership was valued at £5 a year and the other revenues.

At its Dissolution in 1547 the hospital was granted to the City, with a croft called Hildebrond's Spital Croft.

The church was then pulled down but the hospital continued under the name of Ivy Hall or St Edward's Hospital.

There are no remains, the site is partly occupied by Horn's Lane School.

NORWICH - MAGDALEN HOSPITAL AND CHAPEL,
now called the LAZAR HOUSE

Dedicated to the Honour of St Mary Magdalen.

This Hospital and Chapel was built for lepers by Bishop Herbert de Losinga in 1119, he endowed it with many lands and revenues, the benefactors were numerous.

In 1506 it was united to the hospital of St Giles at Bishopsgate, but soon after was separated, different Masters being collated by the Bishop of Norwich who was patron of both.

The hospital consisted of a Master, brethren and sisters, some of whom, in the early days, were lepers.

In 1547 the hospital was granted by Edward VI to Sir Robert Southwell, Master of the Rolls, and John Corbet, for the sum of £276.

The hospital lies a mile north-west out of Magdalen Gates and is just within the boundary of Sprowston. It is now the Lazar House Branch of the Public Library.

It is a most interesting building and must be one of the oldest in Norwich. It comprises of a long hall, now the library, which was once the chapel, with an ante-room and small cloakroom attached, with two cottages. The buildings form an L-shape.

It is well maintained.

NORWICH - MAGDALEN GATE LEPER HOUSE AND CHAPEL

This Leper house was on the east side of the road just outside

Magdalen Gate. Attached to it was a small oratory or chapel.

The founder and date of foundation is unknown.

The chaplains of the leper house lived in a parsonage on the north-west corner of All Saints' churchyard, until its Dissolution.

There was no burial place at the leper house, so those who died were buried in All Saints' churchyard until 1488, when a new chapel was erected at Fyebridge Gate with a burial place adjoining for the lepers.

All Saints' church at Fyebridge stood on the north side of what is now Cowgate, where that thoroughfare joins Magdalen Street.

On March 10th, 1550, the Dean and Chapter of the Cathedral granted the chapel and churchyard of All Saints' to the mayor and citizens for 500 years, at the rent of 4d. a year.

The church was immediately pulled down and the churchyard leased at 6/8d. per year as part of the hospital revenues.

The leper house itself continued for some time after the general Dissolution.

The site of the Leper House is now occupied by the Artichoke Public House.

Just outside Magdalen Gate was the gallows. Every person executed on the gallows at Magdalen Gate had a right of burial in St Margaret's at Fyebridge Gate.

NORWICH - ST SAVIOUR'S HOSPITAL

The Hospital of St Saviour was founded early in the reign of Edward I (1272-1307), by Richard de Brekles, a chaplain.

In 1297 Richard de Coslany, a fishmonger, conveyed to the founder a stall in the bread market, by the stall of the Fraternity of St Mary and St Augustine.

The foundation was confirmed by Edward I in 1304.

Not a lot is known about where the hospital was sited. Some authorities say the site was in the parish of St Michael-at-

Coslany, others place it in St Saviour's parish, in Magdalen Street nearly opposite St Saviour's church.

NORWICH - ST CLEMENT'S HOSPITAL   Infirmary

This Hospital was dedicated to Our Blessed Lady and St Clement.

It is probable that this house was founded by a Bishop of Norwich, as it belonged to the See.

At the Dissolution it became a hospital for such poor as the Bishops thought fit to place here.

The hospital consisted of a Master or custos and several leprous brethren. At first it was for leprous persons, but later on it became an infirmary for old people 'who were infirm and past their labour, who were not fit to be put into common workhouses.'

The lepers here had to live on alms, as there was no regular endowment. Any leper who died in the hospital had a right of burial in St Clement's churchyard, within the City.

The site was outside St Augustine's Gate and was bounded by Waterloo Road, Magpie Road and Starling Road.

There are no remains.

NORWICH - ST PAUL'S HOSPITAL or NORMAN'S SPITAL

Dedicated to St Paul the Apostle, St Paul the Hermit.

The Hospital was founded by the second Bishop of Norwich, Ingalf, the first Prior and Richard de Bellofago or Beaufo of Avranches in Normandy between the year 1118 and 1135.

The hospital buildings and chapel stood to the south of St Paul's church on a site called Cows Croft.

The foundation was confirmed by several charters and bulls. The founders settled the whole croft on the hospital and church and divers parts of it were granted to different tenants at certain yearly rents. This croft was later known as the manor of St Paul and had the gifts of several churches and tithes. These gifts were confirmed by Henry I and ratified by the Pope.

Bishop Eborard granted an indulgence of forty days' pardon to all benefactors. He also made the church parochial and appropriated also for the use of the hospital.

There were about twenty benefactors, including the King and four bishops.

The hospital of St Paul was also known as Norman's Spital. This was derived from Norman, a monk who was the first Master here. In 1198 the rectory of St Paul's was appropriated to the hospital.

The hospital consisted of a Procurator, a master in priest's orders, a wardeness or woman guardian and fourteen men and women. By their many gifts, 'their revenues were sufficient to maintain fourteen poor men and women, decrepit with age or languishing under incurable diseases, and a procurator, custos, or master in priests orders, taken from amongst their own monks at the appointment of the prior and convent, and approved by the bishop. From the year 1198, at which time John of Oxford, Bishop of Norwich, appropriated the rectory of St Paul's church to the hospital, the master served the cure himself or by his chaplain, had all the spiritual jurisdiction over the parish, and proved wills, etc., as official of his exempt jurisdiction.'

In 1429 it was changed to fourteen women, seven of whom were whole sisters, that is, lodged in the hospital, the other seven were half-sisters, who attended divine service, but did not live in. It was also used for the relief and lodging of poor strangers and sick impotent persons, also for the lodging of wayfaring men and women.

In 1565 Agnes Lyon, the last wardress, died. The hospital was then leased to the City for 500 years, at one penny a year. In 1570 this lease was cancelled and a new one was granted without any condition of its being continued as a hospital. The following year the Corporation converted it

[98]

into a bridewell or house of correction for idle and lazy beggars. Thus the site of the hospital fell into the hands of the City, while all the other revenues, together with the right of nomination to the church of St Paul's, remained with the Dean and Chapter of the Cathedral.

There are no remains.

St Paul's church was bombed during the second world war and it has now been completely demolished. On the site of the churchyard now stands a part of the new inner ring road at Barrack Street.

There are no remains of the hospital.

NORWICH - ST BENEDICT'S HOSPITAL
Leper House and Chapel

The Hospital was dedicated to St Benet or Benedict. The founder and date of foundation is unknown.

It was sited outside St Benedict's Gates on the left hand side of the entrance into Barn Road.

It was for lepers and sick people, in charge of whom was a proctor or governor.

At the Dissolution it was not dissolved, but continued as a hospital for some time. During 1584 it was purchased by the City from Messrs. Thomas and Nicholas Layer and it seems apparent that it continued as a hospital until 1697 or just after.

The site is where 'Barn Tavern' now stands, that is, at the corner of Dereham Road and Barn Road. There is nothing left of the original building.

Over St Benedict's Gates, also called Westwick Gates, was an ancient hermitage.

NORWICH - ST BENET'S ALMSHOUSES

Two Almshouses were given to the parish at an early date by Hugh Garezoun or Garzon.

The site was to the south-east of the churchyard of St

Benedict's. Very little is known about them and there are no remains.

NORWICH - ST GILES' HOSPITAL   Leper House and Chapel

This Leper House was founded in the reign of Edward III (1327-1377) by Balderic de Taverham. The original document still exists in the care of the City. It is in old French and dated 1344. The founder, in 1343, settled it on the City.

There is evidence, however, which gives a different origin, for, in 1308 Walter Knot granted to Richard de Ely 'his seven cottages in which the leprous people dwell, lying together without St Giles' Gates, on the north side of the King's highway.'

This was not dissolved at the Dissolution, but continued as a hospital or sick house until 1694.

The site was at the top of Grapes Hill. There is nothing of the original buildings left. The hospital was just outside St Giles' Gate. Over the Gate was a hermitage.

NORWICH - ST STEPHEN'S HOSPITAL
Leper House and Chapel

Dedicated to St Stephen.

This Hospital was founded at an early date, but the date and founder are unknown. It was formerly inhabited by lepers, lazars and lame people.

It was governed by a master, custos or guardian, who before the Dissolution was a person in orders, who officiated daily in the chapel belonging to the house. This master was nominated by the Prior of Horsham St Faith's, on whose See the hospital was built. This nomination was admitted by the Bishop and Mayor of Norwich. The hospital had a foregoer, a person who begged daily outside for the inmates.

This house was not dissolved at the Dissolution but continued as a hospital for some time. However, the seal of this house was altered, and from that time the King presented the masters, and either the bishop or mayor admitted them.

[100]

In 1698 the City leased the tenements, formerly one large house, to John Dunch for 900 years at 2/- per year, payable to the City, and 6/- a year to his Majesty's bailiff.

Nothing remains of the old hospital and the site is occupied by later buildings.

It extended from Chapel Field Road corner, at the ring, and up St Stephen's Road to the chemist's shop.

Over St Stephen's Gate was a hermitage.

NORWICH - ALMSHOUSES IN ST GEORGE IN COLEGATE
Widows' Houses

These poor Widows' Houses were founded by Alice Crome, the exact year being unknown.

Alice Crome herself was a widow and she was buried in St George's church in 1516.

She founded seven almshouses, to be inhabited by poor widows of this parish, and directed that one should be set aside and let to defray the expense of keeping the whole in repair.

The houses were not dissolved at the Dissolution but continued as almshouses for a long time.

The houses were sited in Alms Lane and continued up to St George's Street.

There is nothing remaining of the original buildings.

Also in the parish of Colegate once stood the church of St Margaret at Newbridge. It was anciently known as St Margaret's at Colegate. The inhabitants here nearly all died of the plague in 1349, and the services of the church ceased. The parish was then annexed to St George of Colegate, and the prior and convent converted the churchyard into a garden and the church was turned into a hermitage.

This church stood near the junction of Colegate and St George's Street, near the bridge over the river.

The site is now built on.

[101]

In 1289 there was an anchorage, inhabited by two anchoresses, in the churchyard of St Olive the King and Martyr. This church was commonly called St Tooley's. It was repaired in 1504 and demolished in 1546. It stood near the corner of Pitt Street and Cherry Lane. In 1546 the parish was consolidated with St George's, Colegate.

NORWICH - ST STEPHEN'S ALMSHOUSES

Two brothers, John and Walter Danyel, built there, Almshouses for the poor in 1418. They were not dissolved at the Dissolution.

The houses were in St Catherine's and St Stephen's in Newgate. Walter Danyel also gave another four houses in this parish to the poor.

They were sited on the south-west side of Surrey Street and ran nearly to the corner of All Saints' Green.

There are no remains of the original buildings.

OUTWELL, NEAR WISBECH, THE HERMITAGE OF ST CHRISTOPHER

Near St Clement's church at Outwell was a Hermitage and Chapel dedicated to St Christopher.

It was in existence in 1348, but nothing else is known.

The site adjoins the main road, but there is nothing above the foundations.

PENTNEY PRIORY, NEAR SWAFFHAM   Augustinian Canons

Dedicated to the Holy Trinity, the Blessed Virgin Mary and St Mary Magdalen.

Robert de Vallibus or Vaux founded this priory in the time of William the Conqueror for the souls of Agnes his wife and their children. He endowed it with the advowsons of six churches, with the hermitage of Welney, as well as lands and liberties.

These grants were augmented by his descendants and other

noble benefactors. In 1291 it possessed land and property in 34 parishes in Norfolk to the value of £67.17.7¾d., and in Chedison in Suffolk 4/2d.

In 1468 the priory of Wormegay was united and consolidated to this priory by Walter Hart, 27th Bishop of Norwich, with the consent of John, Earl of Northumberland, patron of Wormegay priory.

Just before the Dissolution it possessed lands and rents in about 41 parishes, with 11 manors and interests in the patronages of 17 churches.

The priory consisted of a Prior and 13 canons. They all subscribed to the King's supremacy. It was valued at approximately £200.

Within the precincts of this priory were buried the nobility of the area.

The remains are down a lane, about two miles to the southwest of Pentney. There is little more than the foundations, except for the gatehouse, which is one of the finest in the county. It was built in the late 14th century.

PETERSTONE PRIORY, BURNHAM OVERY
Augustinian Canons

Dedicated to St Peter.

This was originally a medieval Hospital, but later became a branch priory of Walsingham Monastery. It was founded by a member of the Cheney family.

At the Dissolution it went to the Crown and was valued with Walsingham.

The slight remains are mixed up with the farm buildings of Peterstone Farm. There is very little to see.

PRIOR THORN'S MANOR, SWAFFHAM   Cistercian Monks

This House was founded in the reign of Henry II (1154-1189).

The Abbot of Sawtree or Saltrey, in Huntingdonshire, held

a manor and land in Swaffham, given to Sawtree Abbey by Warine de Bassingbourn and Alan of Swaffham.

In the house belonging to their manor, the monks of Sawtree placed two or three brethren, mainly for the reception of pilgrims on their way to Walsingham. This manor was subordinate to Sawtree Abbey until the Dissolution.

In 1291 it was valued at £17.9.8d., with possessions in six parishes in Norfolk. In 1537 it was granted to Sir Richard Williams, alias Cromwell.

Nothing remains above the foundations. The site is about two miles west of Swaffham.

RACHENESS LEPER HOUSE AND CHURCH, SOUTHACRE

Dedicated to St Bartholomew.

This Leper House and Church was founded in the time of Henry II. Herbert de Sudacra and William his heir gave to the priory of Castleacre certain lands in Palgrave, Burstall and Southacre, and at Racheness a church was founded and a leper house built for the soul of the founder and Hugoline his wife. The brother of the founder, Alan de Palgrave, confirmed and augmented the endowment of the brethren of Racheness.

In the reign of Henry III, William de Palgrave and Hamon Cook of Acre were mentioned as benefactors.

The church was also used for parochial purposes, but went to decay after the Dissolution.

There is nothing remaining above the foundations. The site is still called St Bartholomew's Hill.

RUDHAM (EAST), HOSPITAL OF BOYCODESWADE IN COXFORD, NEAR FAKENHAM

Dedicated to St Andrew.

This Hospital was built by Hervey Beleth or Belet, Lord of East Rudham, around 1181 at a place called Boycodeswade.

Here he placed a secular canon to serve God therein forever, for his own soul, for that of his wife Emma, his mother, and for the souls of his brothers, parents and ancestors.

He endowed it with the lordship of East Rudham and with lands in Gayton, Marham, Syderstone and Barmer.

The hospital consisted of a warden, chaplain and 13 poor people, under the government of the Prior of Coxford. (Augustinian Canons).

In 1491 Robert Sharington, the chaplain, left money to the people in this hospital.

In 1534 the stipend to the chaplain here was £5.6.8d. The revenue for supporting 12 poor people in the hospital was valued at £14.13.4d. The hospital was granted to Thomas Howard, Duke of Norfolk, in 1537. It later went to the Townshend family.

The site was to the side of Coxford Priory, there are no remains.

RUSHFORD COLLEGE AND COLLEGIATE CHURCH, NEAR THETFORD

Dedicated to the honour of Almighty God, Our Blessed Lady, St John the Evangelist and All Saints.

Sir Edmund de Gonville, a priest, also founder of Gonville Hall in Cambridge, and one of the founders of the Black Friars in Cambridge, being the patron and rector of Rushford, appropriated the church to the college, the foundation of which was completed in 1326-1342. It consisted of several lands and revenues, with the churches of Rushford and Larling and a manor in Elveden.

The canons officiated in the church. Their dormitory, refectory and chapel were on the south side of the churchyard. The college was governed by statute, confirmed by Bishop Percy, in a visit made in 1360.

The collegiate church was subject to episcopal and archidiaconal jurisdiction, the master or custos being installed by the archdeacon.

In 1500 it consisted of a Master and six brethren, two chantry priests, seven children and one clerk.

Just before the Dissolution the college possessed, in the parish of Rushford, 200 acres of arable land, 8 acres of meadow with liberty and pasture for 1,300 sheep, valued at £27.2.11½d. In 1534 the total valuation was £85.15.0½d.

The Master and five brethren subscribed to the King's supremacy at the Dissolution.

The site of the college with all its lands, revenues, etc., was granted to Henry, Earl of Surrey, in 1541. In 1545 they were alienated to Thomas, Duke of Norfolk, and after his attainder were granted in 1550 to Sir John Cheke.

The college was placed just to the south of the church. It was once surrounded by a moat; this is now partly filled up. Part of the original college buildings can still be seen incorporated in the rectory since built.

Sir Edmund was also founder of Caius College, Cambridge.

ST WINWALOE'S PRIORY, NEAR WEREHAM

Alien for Benedictine Monks

Dedicated to St Winwaloe.

St Winwaloe was a British saint, about 550 AD. His body is enshrined in the Abbey of Mounstrol.

The priory was founded before 1199 by one of the Earls of Clare, to whom the patronage belonged.

The priory is on the same scale as Castle Acre. It was once a cell to the Abbey of Mounstrol in France, but the Abbey sold it in 1321 to Hugh Scarlet, who sold it yet again to Elizabeth de Burgo. In 1336 this lady, the sister of the Earl of Clare, obtained a licence to assign lands and rents here, and in the adjoining parishes to West Dereham Abbey, also to find a chaplain in the chapel of St Winwaloe to celebrate Divine Service for the souls of the said Elizabeth, and the Earl of Clare forever.

In 1291 it was valued at £7.2.8d., with possessions in three parishes. At the Dissolution it was valued with West Dereham Abbey. It was granted to Thomas Gaybon and William Mynn in 1556.

There are some remains one-and-half miles north of Wereham. These can be seen in the walls of Winwall House, a farmhouse on the site.

SHERINGHAM PRIORY CELL   Augustinian Canons

Dedicated to All Saints.

This was a Priory cell appropriated to the Abbey of Nutley in Buckinghamshire. Both the cell and abbey were founded in 1162. Walter Gifford, the second Earl of Buckingham, and his wife Ermengard, founded the abbey, and at the same time appropriated to it the parish church of All Saints', Sheringham, which was served by a canon of Nutley.

Certain rents due from Middleton (King's Lynn) to Nutley Abbey were made payable at Sheringham.

At the Dissolution the cell was granted in 1543 to the Dean and Chapter of Christ's College, Oxford. This was later revoked and it was leased by the Crown to Francis Guybon and others.

The cell stood adjacent to the churchyard, but nothing remains of this. The church of All Saints' is still used and is in a good state of repair. The church is in Upper Sheringham.

SHOULDHAM PRIORY, NEAR MARHAM
Gilbertine Canons and Nuns

Dedicated to the Holy Cross and the Blessed Virgin Mary.

The canons here followed the Rule of St Augustine, and the nuns that of St Benedict.

This Priory was founded by Jeffrey Fitzpiers, Earl of Essex, in the reign of Richard I (1189-1199), about the year 1190. He appropriated it with several manors and six churches, with the consent of John de Gray, Lord Chief Justice and 5th Bishop of Norwich from 1200-1222.

[107]

Henry III (1216-1272), and Edward I (1272-1307), confirmed and extended the privileges.

The monastery was valued in 1291 at £207.7.9½d., made up of property in 26 parishes in Norfolk to the value of £199.17.1½d., and property in the diocese of London to the value of £7.10.8d. There were many titled benefactors to the priory, many of whom are buried here.

In 1538 the Prior, nine canons and seven nuns, surrendered to the King's supremacy.

It remained in the hands of the Crown until 1553, when it was then sold to Thomas Mildmay for £1049.9.4½d.

The site is south of Abbey Farm. Nothing remains above the foundations.

At All Saints' Church, Shouldham, outside the south transept, is a coffin lid with a foliated cross. This is said to have come from Shouldham Priory.

SLEVESHOLM PRIORY, METHWOLD   Cluniac Monks

Dedicated to the Blessed Virgin Mary and St Giles.

This Priory was founded by William, the third Earl of Surrey, in the reign of King Stephen (1135-1154). It was a cell subject to Castleacre Priory.

The Prior of Slevesholm was always to be a monk elected by and out of Castleacre.

In 1291 it was valued at £1.10.7½d., with land in Slevesholm only. In 1428 it was valued at £1.15.7½d. At the Dissolution it was valued with Castleacre. In 1538 it was granted to Osbert Mundefort of Feltwell.

The site is in an isolated position in the fens, some distance from the parish church of Methwold. Nothing remains above the foundations.

SNORING PARVA LAZAR HOUSE, NEAR FAKENHAM

Somewhere in the parish of Little Snoring, at a place called Queengate, was situated a Lazar House. It is mentioned in

[108]

the will of Alexander, rector of Snoring Parva, in the year 1380. Other than this, nothing is known.

Another unsolved problem relates to the church of St Andrew at Little Snoring. Here a church was begun in Early Norman days and then left unfinished. Immediately to the north of the first church, also in its beginnings still Norman, was built another church.

SOMERTON (WEST) LEPER HOSPITAL, NEAR WINTERTON

This Hospital was founded by Rannulph de Glanville, Lord Chief Justice of England and founder of Butley Priory in Suffolk, having been given a part of the lordship of West Somerton by Henry II (1154-1189). His son-in-law, William de Auberville, further endowed it with the advowson of West Somerton church in 1235. Other benefactors included William de Gyselham and his wife Isabel in 1277.

The hospital was subordinate to the priory of Butley. From the manor of West Somerton, £10 was appropriated to support two canons in the monastery at Butley, to serve God and to pray for the soul of the founder.

The value of the hospital in 1291 was given at £3.11.3d.

This hospital cared for thirteen leprous persons.

In 1552 it was granted to Edward Lord Clinton.

The site is to the north-east of the parish church of St Mary's. There are no remains above the foundations.

SPORLE PRIORY, NEAR SWAFFHAM
Alien for Benedictine Monks

It is not known for certain who founded this Alien Priory.

It was a cell to the Abbey of St Florence at Saumers, in the diocese of Angers in the province of Anjou in France. During the wars with France it was in the hands of the Crown.

Sporle and Palgrave churches were appropriated to the priory and also the tithes of Sporle and Palgrave Parva.

[109]

In 1291 it was valued at 8/6d., with possessions in four parishes. It was dissolved by the Parliament of Leicester in 1416. It was granted to Joan, Queen Dowager of England, for her lifetime. In 1440 it was given by Henry VI to Eton College.

The site, with a few remains, are south of the parish church.

STANHOE PILGRIMS' CHAPEL, NEAR DOCKING

The Chapel was dedicated to St Peter.

The name of the founder and date of foundation are unknown.

It was used mainly by the pilgrims going to and from the Shrine of Our Lady at Walsingham.

It fell into decay after the Dissolution.

The site is at a place called Chapel Field, a few hundred yards east of the parish church. The foundations can be traced.

THETFORD

Thetford was once a very prosperous and important town. It had thirteen parish churches in the 11th century and twenty in the late 14th century, seventeen of which have now gone to decay. The cathedral of East Anglia was here from 1075-1094, before the See was moved to Norwich.

Besides these there were six monastic establishments and seven smaller ones, making thirteen in all, being four priories, a nunnery, a medieval college and seven smaller types of medieval hospitals. At the Dissolution the prosperity of all its monastic institutions were completely brought to a standstill.

Many of the remains are mixed up with later buildings and it is difficult at times to ascertain their sites. There are, however, remains of some of the larger monastic establishments.

Since the second world war, Thetford has been turned into an overspill town with a great movement of population from London, with large council estates and light industry.

[110]

THETFORD - BENEDICTINE NUNNERY

Dedicated to St George.

This Monastery was originally founded for monks by Uvius, the first Abbot of Bury, just after 1020, to commemorate the great local battle that was fought between St. Edmund and the Danes.

The founder placed here a few Benedictine monks, and for more than 150 years it remained a cell to Bury Abbey.

In 1176 the Abbot of Bury, Hugh de Norwold, brought the nuns from Lyng to here, and from that time the monastery continued as a nunnery.

The church of St George, which was parochial, in which the monks had officiated, was then made conventual (1176) and the revenues from this time received many additions.

The list of benefactors to the nunnery was considerable and included many titled people.

In 1420 the convent consisted of a Prioress, sub-prioress, third-prioress, refectoress, infirmeress and five nuns.

At the time of the Dissolution there was a Prioress and ten nuns. In 1534 the value was given as £40.11.2½d., with possessions in about 25 parishes.

In 1540 it was granted to Sir Richard Fulmerstone of Ipswich.

It is recorded that one night in 1305, John Cot, chaplain to the nuns, broke bounds with two clerks to 'gossip' with Joan de Fieldon.

The site of the nunnery is off the road to Euston, about three-quarters of a mile from the centre of the town. It was quite large. The church, with a south transept, is now a large barn. It is worth a visit.

THETFORD - PRIORY   Cluniac Monks

Dedicated to the Blessed Virgin Mary and St Andrew.

Roger Bigod, Earl of the East Angles, and his wife Alice, founded this Priory in 1104. He was advised by the Bishop of

Norwich, Herbert de Losinga, and assisted by King Henry I and Lanzo, Abbot of Lewes. It was dependent on the foreign Abbey of Cluni.

At first there were twelve Cluniac monks, with Malgod the Prior. They were placed in the church of Saint Mary the Great on the Suffolk side of the river.

They arrived on 4th July, 1104, amongst great rejoicing. For three years the monks laboured, building a monastery next to the church. Then Malgod was recalled, and Prior Stephen was sent from Lewes to replace him. He took one look at the building and disapproved of the site. He then stirred up the founder, Roger Bigod, and King Henry, who was at the time staying at Thetford, and it was agreed to remove the monastery to a more open space on the Norfolk side of the river.

This was done, and the monastery duly built. The monks removed to their new monastery on St Martin's Day, 1114.

The founder died in 1107 and, as he had directed that his body was to be buried in the monastery, the Prior was very angry on finding out the Bishop of Norwich had possession of it. The Bishop was determined to bury it at Norwich. The Prior did his utmost to get the body back, but to no avail. The Bishop insisted that the founder had directed to be buried at Norwich and the Prior of Thetford was obliged to submit.

There seems to have been no great affection on the part of either Prior or Bishop for the founder, Roger Bigod, so perhaps it was just simply gain. Bishop Herbert was anxious to secure so valuable a source of revenue as the celebration of masses, the offerings, etc., of so great and wealthy a man, as would certainly have brought to his own foundation at Norwich, and the Prior probably had the same designs for Thetford.

As this was an alien priory, it was always seized during the wars with France. In 1375, however, the Earl of Norfolk procured a licence to make it denizen from Edward III (1327-1377).

The revenues from this priory were considerable, with a list of nearly 40 benefactors, including the names of kings, queens, earls and many other titled people. There were nearly 50 churches, or portions, appropriated to the priory, besides 23 manors.

At the foundation there was a prior and 12 monks. This increased to a Prior and 17 monks.

In 1540 the Prior and 13 monks signed the surrender.

Many privileges were enjoyed at this priory and it obtained considerable celebrity from the miraculous image of the Blessed Virgin in her chapel.

There were also many relics, such as the purple robe of Our Lord, of the Virgin's girdle, of the Lord's sepulchre, of the rock of Calvary, of the sepulchre of St Mary, of the Lord's manger, of the earth found in the sepulchre of Saint John the Evangelist, of St George, of the hair of St Agnes, of the wooden coffin of St Edmund, and also of St Etheldreda and many others. No doubt all a good source of income for the priory.

One of the priors of Thetford was murdered in 1248. This prior declared himself to be a relation of the Queen and had assumed airs of pride from this. He began to indulge himself in immoderate eating and drinking, forgetting his matins devotion, didn't bother to be present at Mass and seldom appeared at canonical hours, in general he acted in a manner unbecoming to his position.

In time a dispute arose between the Prior and one of his monks, a Welshman by birth.

The Prior was endeavouring to send this monk back to Clugny, from where he had come, but not from charity, from hate. The poor monk excused himself on reasonable grounds and refused to go.

The Prior swore horribly that he would send the monk on a pilgrimage with the script and wallet. At this, the monk, in passion, drew a knife and plunged it into the Prior's stomach

[113]

and then did it repeatedly three or four times into the then lifeless body.

The monk was seized and committed to prison. When the King heard of the murder he ordered the murderer to be chained and, after being deprived of his eyes, to be thrown into the lowest dungeon in the castle at Norwich.

The obits of 7 people were annually kept here and returned at the value of £3.9.0d.

Every year alms to the value of £8.10.0d. were distributed to the poor. In 1291 the value was given at £123.12.5d., with possessions in over 60 parishes. In 1534 the value seems to have been between £300-£400. In 1540 it was granted to Thomas Howard, Duke of Norfolk.

The remains are extensive and of great interest. The church was 248 feet long and 123 feet across at the transepts. At the crossing the Norman tower was 36 feet square. There were two towers at the west end.

The plan is like that of the 10th century Abbey of Cluny.

It was the third largest monastic church in the county with Norwich and Walsingham being first and second.

The remains are looked after by the Ministry of Works and are sited at the end of Minstergate. They are well worth a visit.

THETFORD - PRIORY OF CANONS OF THE
HOLY SEPULCHRE   Augustinian Canons

Dedicated to the Honour of God, the Holy Sepulchre and the Holy Cross.

The Priory was founded about 1139 by William de Warren, the third Earl Warren of Surrey. King Stephen (1135-1154) gave the demeans of the borough of Thetford and the advowsons of all the churches on the Suffolk side of the river to Earl Warren. He immediately founded a monastery and church, endowing them with all he had received from the King.

[114]

After completing the foundations he joined in the crusade against the infidels and was killed in Palestine in 1148.

His only daughter, Isabel, confirmed her father's gifts, which were further augmented by the succeeding Earls.

Just before the Dissolution the Priory consisted of a Prior and six canons. They all subscribed to the King's supremacy in 1534. Four years later the Prior signed the surrender.

The total value in 1291 was £20.0.1¼d., with property in many parishes.

At the Dissolution in 1534 the value was given as £39.6.8d., with one estimate given as £49.18.1d. In 1540 it was granted to Sir Richard Fulmerstone.

The remains are in Brandon Road. There is little detail left. The west wall is still there, but the chancel has disappeared.

THETFORD - PRIORY OF BLACK FRIARS   Dominican Friars

Dedicated to the Holy Trinity, St Mary and All Saints.

Probably founded in 1335 by John Plantagenet, 7th Earl of Warren and Surrey, Lord of Thetford; and Henry, Earl of Lancaster. They placed the friars in the buildings here, with the advice of Sir Edmund Gonville, a priest (*See* Rushford College).

The patronage of the priory was in the hands of the lords of the borough of Thetford and they nominated the Priors.

In 1347 Henry, Duke of Lancaster, gave them the site of Domus Dei, a medieval hospital. This was situated between the friars' cloisters and the High Street. Shortly afterwards the revenues of the hospital were given to the priory.

Before the Black Friars took over this site it was occupied by the ancient parish church of St Mary, then the residence of the Cluniac monks for a time.

By 1370 the friars had considerably enlarged their precincts. This was due to various benefactions and purchases they had made.

[115]

In this church, when it had been the Cathedral of the See, Arfast, the Bishop of Thetford was buried in 1084. John of Gaunt was a benefactor to the priory about the year 1386.

The site of the priory and hospital was granted to Sir Richard Fulmerstone.

The remains are built into the Grammar School, London Road.

THETFORD - PRIORY OF AUSTIN FRIARS

Augustinian Friars

Dedicated to St Augustine.

These friars were brought to Thetford in 1387 by John of Gaunt, Duke of Lancaster. He placed them here in a cloister and built them a church within the entrenchments of the old Danish earthworks, which was part of the founder's lordship and demesne. (Castle Hill).

He also granted them the parish church of St John on the Suffolk side of the river, where a friar was placed as master of the lepers there. This leper hospital helped the friars to further support their fraternity as basically they were mendicants or a begging fraternity.

There were many benefactors to the priory. In 1407 they enlarged their conventual church and buildings at Castle Hill. Henry IV (1399-1413) licensed them to build a hermitage at the west end of the church, which was next to the street. Here they received alms for the profit and support of the fraternity.

The fraternity consisted generally of a Prior and about six brethren. In 1538 only the prior and two friars signed the surrender.

In 1540 the site of the priory, the church of St John and all the land belonging to the friars were granted to Sir Richard Fulmerstone.

None of the conventual buildings remain above the foundations. The site is between Castle Lane and the river.

In 1807 the foundations were removed and coffins containing the remains of two benefactresses were discovered. These bodies were re-interred near the same spot, with inscriptions. The first was Dame Elizabeth, daughter of John de Herling, wife of Sir Thomas Hengrave of Suffolk. She died in 1402. The second was Dame Margery, daughter of Sir Thomas Jenny and wife of John de Herling, Lord of Herling, and afterwards wife to Sir John Tudenham. She died in 1412.

THETFORD - COLLEGE OF ST MARY

This College was dedicated to St Mary and the Church to St Bartholomew.

Sometime during the 12th century a Guild was established at Thetford, dedicated to the Virgin Mary, consisting of brethren and sisters with a chaplain or priest of its own.

In the time of Edward I (1272-1307), Sir Gilbert de Pickenham converted the Guild into a College for a master and fellows. He also built them a mansion house and chapel, and endowed them with lands and tenements. He also invested the patronage and nomination of the fellows, in the Mayor and commonalty of the borough.

In 1392 Richard II licensed them to purchase other lands on condition that they found a chantry in the chapel of St Bartholomew in the Guildhall. This was to be served by the fellows of the college.

The college had many benefactors, the obits of three being observed here annually. In 1446 the fraternity had to elect two chamberlains to receive the revenues due to the college, as they had increased so much.

The college consisted of a Master and fellows. In 1337 there were about 36 in residence, and in 1416 about 45. The Guild or fraternity of St Mary also formed a part of this institution, also with the tabernacle of the Virgin Mary.

The value given in 1534 was only £5.9.7d.

The site of the college and chapel and 80 acres of land, rights and messuages in Thetford and Croxton were granted in 1547 to Thomas, Duke of Norfolk, and after his attainder, to Richard Fulmerstone.

All the collegiate buildings and chapel were destroyed at the Dissolution. There are no remains.

THETFORD - DOMUS DEI OR MEDIEVAL HOSPITAL

The foundation of this Hospital has been ascribed to William II (1087-1100). He had at the time the Lordship of Thetford, probably in 1094.

At first the house was well endowed, but John, Earl of Warren and Surrey, gave the revenues to the canons. These revenues, which came from 864 acres of land, were transferred to the canons to find two chaplains to say Mass for the soul of the founder and also for the maintenance of three poor people for forty weeks in each year. These three poor people had to wash the feet of pilgrims who lodged there when on their way to the great shrine.

The patron of the hospital in 1347, Henry, Duke of Lancaster, granted the site and endowment to the Dominicans. They enlarged their monastery with part of the site, and reserved the hospital for one or two of the friars to beg in.

After the Dissolution the whole site went to Sir Richard Fulmerstone.

The whole of the hospital went to decay after the Dissolution, with the monastery of the Dominicans.

THETFORD - LEPER HOUSE OF ST JOHN

John of Gaunt, Duke of Lancaster, around 1387 gave the parish church of St John to the Augustinian friars. These friars placed some of their brethren inside, and also some lepers to beg at this entrance to the town (*See* Priory of Austin Friars).

It was then called the chapel, hermitage or leper house of St John.

The parish in which this hospital stood was united to that of the Holy Trinity, the patronage however belonged to the

[118]

successive lords of the manor of Thetford, until the Dissolution. In 1540 it was granted to Richard Fulmerstone.

The site lay on the Suffolk side of the river.

All the buildings were destroyed at the Dissolution. Nothing remains above the foundations.

THETFORD - HOSPITAL AND CHURCH OF ST MARGARET

This Church and Hospital was situated on the Suffolk side of the river. It was parochial in the time of Edward the Confessor (1042-1066) but was annexed to St Mary's during the reign of Richard II (1377-1399). St Mary's belonged to the See of Ely.

Soon after the uniting of these two parishes, St Margaret's church was assigned to a hospital or house of lepers in 1390.

In 1390 the Bishop offered an indulgence of 40 days pardon to all who would become benefactors to the poor men and lepers in the hospital of St Margaret.

It was not dissolved until the reign of Edward VI (1547-1553) and was granted to Sir Richard Fulmerstone.

The site is near the town ditch on the left-hand side of Elveden Road. There are no remains above the foundations, but many human bones have been excavated from time to time.

THETFORD - ST JOHN THE BAPTIST HOSPITAL AND CHURCH FOR LEPERS

The founder of this Leper Hospital is thought to have been Roger Bigod, Earl of Norfolk, sometime during the reign of Henry I (1100-1135). It was sited in the parish of St Cuthbert near St Cuthbert's cross.

In the reign of Henry III (1216-1272) John, Earl of Warren and Surrey, suppressed it and founded the hospital of St Mary Magdalen. He then removed the brethren from the old house to the new.

[119]

The Guild of St John the Baptist was also transferred to the new hospital.

There is nothing to see above the foundations.

THETFORD - ST MARY MAGDALEN'S HOSPITAL AND CHURCH FOR LEPERS

This Hospital and Church was founded by John, Earl of Warren and Surrey sometime during the reign of Henry III (1216-1272). He endowed it with lands and revenues and appropriated the chapel of St Mary Magdalen to the use of the Master and brethren.

At the same time he brought the brethren from the dissolved leper hospital of St John the Baptist and settled them here in St Mary's. Just after 1361 the patronage went to the King, Edward III. He in turn granted it to the mayor and commonalty of Thetford, who nominated the custos or master until the Dissolution.

In 1534 it was valued at £1.13.6d. It was granted to Sir William Fermour in 1549. He released it to Sir Richard Fulmerstone in the same year.

The site is just off the Norwich road at the northern edge of the town. There are no remains above the foundation.

THETFORD - ST MARY'S AND ST JULIAN'S HOSPITAL AND CHAPEL

The Hospital was dedicated to St Mary and the Chapel to St Julian. The foundation of the hospital is ascribed to Henry I (1100-1135) and the patronage went with the lordship of Thetford.

It seems to have been used for the reception of poor travellers and pilgrims.

The chapel of St Julian was destroyed just after the Dissolution and the hospital of St Mary was pulled down in 1777.

They were sited on the north-east side of Bridge Street, near the bridge itself, on the Norfolk side of the river.

[120]

THETFORD - HOSPITAL SCHOOL AND ALMSHOUSE

There was a very early school in Thetford. It seems to have been fairly large as is evident from the many collations to it by the Bishop, in whose donation it was.

It seems to have been in existence in 1328. John de Morton was Master in 1329, and he was admitted by the Bishop.

In 1540 it was dissolved and the property was granted to Sir Richard Fulmerstone in 1566.

Sir Richard re-founded it the same year and built a free school upon the site of the Trinity church and of the Black Friars church, formerly the cathedral.

In 1610, with the assistance of Lord Chief Justice Coke, a corporate body was founded, 'The master and fellows of the school and hospital of Thetford.' This consisted of a master, in priest's orders, an usher and four poor people in an almshouse.

The remains of Blackfriars are built into the Grammar School, London Road.

By the churchyard of St Mary are the Fulmerstone Almshouses, founded in 1610.

The church of St Mary (the Great) was an old Saxon church which was demolished when Thetford became head of the See, and the cathedral was built on its site.

THOMPSON, NEAR WATTON   College of Secular Canons

The College was dedicated to St Martin, the Holy Virgin and All Saints.

This college of Thompson is said to have been originated in the time of Edward I (1272-1307) from the Boutetort family who were lords of this place.

In 1349 Sir Thomas de Shardelowe and Sir John de Shardelowe, his brother, endowed the college with the parish church at Thompson (St Martin), and with several manors and rents. These two brothers are deemed to be the founders. Sir Thomas gave his arms to the college and these can be seen to this day

[121]

carved on the Miserere seats in the chancel. His remains are buried in the chapel of St James' to the south of the nave.

On 28th April, 1369, Joan, the widow of Sir John de Shardelowe, took upon herself the vow of chastity and became a religious votary in the college, where she died.

At the Dissolution, they possessed various lands, including a manor in Thompson, 290 acres of arable land, 32 acres of meadow land and the liberty of foldage and pasture for 800 sheep in the parish. They also possessed various lands in other parishes and also the manors of Broadcar in Shropham and Citye Campes in Cambridgeshire.

The college consisted of a Master and five secular canons. In 1534 the Master and four canons submitted to the King's supremacy. The value at this time was given as £52.15.7½d. In 1542 the property was granted to Sir Edmund Knevet.

In the church of St Martin's, in the chancel, were eleven stalls belonging to the Fellows of the College. They have the Tudor Rose as elbow pieces. Only four of the Misereres remain, two bearing the arms of Shardelowe, one the head of a Bishop and the fourth a head of of a woman.

The site of the conventual buildings is several hundred yards to the south of the parish church. It is now called the College Farmhouse.

TOFT MONKS PRIORY, NEAR BECCLES
Alien for Benedictine Monks
The Priory was dedicated to St Margaret.

Henry I (1100-1135) granted the principal manor of Toft to Robert de Bellomont, Earl of Mellent in Normandy and of Leicester in England. He in turn granted it to the Benedictine Abbey of St Peter and St Paul de Pratellis or Preaux, in Normandy.

The cell at Toft received several lands and privileges and also with two parts of the appropriation of the parish church of St Margaret's at Toft.

[122]

It is thought that some monks were sent from the mother house in Normandy to this cell.

In 1269 the priory received a substantial addition to its endowments from Humphrey de Worlingham. The value of this alien priory was given as £44.17.4½d. in 1291, with possessions in three parishes.

Although alien, it was dedicated to St Margaret, the same as its appropriated church, and was suppressed by the Parliament of Leicester in 1415. It was granted for life to Sir Thomas Erpingham in 1418. After his death it was granted to the Carthusians at Witham in Somersetshire, then to Eton College in 1431.

In 1461 Edward IV presented it to King's College in Cambridge. The Provost and Fellows of King's College are still lords of the manor and patrons of the rectory.

WALSINGHAM, LITTLE — Priory of Austin Canons

Dedicated to the Annunciation of the Blessed Virgin Mary.

About five years before the Norman Conquest, probably in 1061, Richeldis, the young widow of Ricoldie de Fervaquers, Lady of the Manor of Walsingham Parva, prayed that she might undertake some special work to honour Our Blessed Lady.

In response to this prayer, the Blessed Virgin led her in spirit to Nazareth, there to show her the Holy House, scene of the Annunciation. Our Lady commanded the young widow to mark well the length and breadth and to build an exact counterpart at Walsingham.

Thus Richeldis built the first little chapel to the honour of that saint, similar to the Sancta Casa at Nazareth. It stood here at Walsingham for nearly 500 years and was the focus of medieval devotion until it was destroyed in the sixteenth century.

The young widow's son, Geoffrey de Fervaques (born 1060, died 1130) soon after the Conquest endowed it with lands, tithes, rents and services. He also founded a Priory of Austin Canons, to which he gave the chapel of St Mary, founded by his mother. He also built for the canons a priory church.

All these gifts were confirmed by his successors and by several kings, popes and bishops.

Considerable wealth was derived from the image of Our Lady of Walsingham and many thousands of subjects, including kings and queens of England, crowded here to lay their offerings and to make vows before her. The chapel which housed the image was a separate building from the church, and it housed a resident Canon within it to receive the many offerings.

William, the brother of Henry II (1154-1189) was a great benefactor to the priory, and Henry III made at least eleven pilgrimages to Walsingham between 1226 and 1272. Amongst his gifts were forty oaks for the work of the church, and two years later he gave another twenty trees. He also gave a yearly offering of 40/- and many smaller gifts of wax and tapers. His son, Edward I, was a pilgrim on at least twelve occasions.

For many years the road to Walsingham became one of England's main highways, marked by pilgrim chapels and hostelries.

The Milky Way was re-named the Walsingham Way. It was said to point across the heavens the route to England's Nazareth in the Holy Land of Walsingham.

In the chapel of the Blessed Mary was a chantry priest for the souls of Edward I and Edward II, and of Sir John Ovidale. There was also another chaplain to pray for the souls of John Marshall and Anne his wife.

The last King of England to make a pilgrimage to Walsingham was Henry VIII. He walked barefoot to the Shrine from the Slipper Chapel. The endowment of the priory comprised of the patronage or interest in thirteen churches, with fourteen manors and with the cells of Flitcham and Peterstone.

In 1291 the value was given as £79.2.6¾d., with property

in at least 86 parishes in Norfolk. In 1534 the total amount was given as £652.3.11¾d., Henry VIII sold the site of the Priory in 1539 to Thomas Sydney for £90, although much of the property went to Sir Thomas Gresham. On 18th September, 1534, the Prior and Canons of Walsingham signed the Act of the King's supremacy, making Walsingham one of the first religious houses to submit. At this time there was a Prior and twenty-one canons in residence. In 1536 the sub-prior and sixteen others tried to get the priory re-established, but were condemned for treason. They were put on trial at Norwich Castle and early in 1537 eleven were condemned to death. There was nothing proved against them at their trial other than unwise talk. They were to be hanged, drawn and quartered.

Five were executed in the Castle ditch at Norwich, two at Great Yarmouth and two at King's Lynn. The sub-prior, Nicholas Myleham and George Gisborough, were executed at Walsingham on 30th May 1537, on the hill overlooking the Priory on the west. It is still known as 'Martyrs Field.'

In June 1538, the image of Our Lady of Walsingham was taken away to London and burnt at Chelsea in the presence of Cromwell, Lord Privy Seal. Later in the same year, on 4th August, the Priory was handed over to the King's Commissioners. The little chapel was torn down and the priory church stripped of all its lead and furniture. The windows, doors, glass, iron, slates, etc., were sold in lots for a total of £55.15.11d.

On the east side of the High Street is the gatehouse to the Priory. Admission may be gained by the payment of a small fee. Inside the grounds the most impressive piece is the east wall of the church, with a very large window and two turrets. The church was originally 250 feet long. Near the remains of this east wall are two 'Wishing Wells.' There is a legend that persons drinking these waters will obtain any wish made while drinking it. The wells are still there, side by side, with the

[125]

water within arm's reach, although not a very appetising sight, being a nice shade of green. Near the twin wells is a path leading to a stone bridge over a stream. Near this bridge was once the house of Gilbert de Clare, possibly the original Manor House in which Richeldis lived.

Fragments of Roman and Saxon pottery and other evidence of occupation were found here in the vicinity during the 1955 and 1961 excavations.

The National Catholic Shrine of Our Lady of Walsingham is at present the Slipper Chapel, a mile from the Friday Market Place going south.

The Anglo-Catholic Shrine was built in 1931-1937 in Walsingham. It is an uninteresting building from the outside, being built of brick and partly whitewashed. There is not enough evidence to justify the claim that this shrine stands where the Holy House had been. The village of Walsingham and the surrounding countryside is most interesting and well worth a visit.

According to Erasmus, in the chapel of St Lawrence by the Wells was exhibited a relic. It was the joint of a man's finger, and believed to be St. Peter the Apostle's. On the high altar, enclosed in crystal, was kept 'the sacred milk of the Blessed Virgin.'

WALSINGHAM (LITTLE), - PRIORY OF GREY FRIARS
Franciscan Friars

Dedicated to St Mary.

This House of Grey Friars was founded by Elizabeth de Burgh or Burgo, Countess of Clare, in the reign of Edward III about 1347.

The friars met with great opposition from the nearby Augustinian Canons, and there were constant quarrels and disputes between the two monasteries, which raged to the time of the Dissolution. It seems the Austin Canons were mainly at fault, and they did all they could to injure their opponents.

[126]

Although this order professed poverty, it seems they were endowed with several lands, gardens and houses. It never became a wealthy house, however, and was completely overshadowed by the better-known Priory of Austin Canons.

These friars derived a large proportion of their revenues by entertaining pilgrims.

At the time of the Dissolution, Giles Coventry was Prior. The priory was surrendered in 1538 to the Bishop of Dover. It was valued at only £3. In 1544 the property was granted to John Eyre.

In 1526 an anchoress resided in or near the priory.

The ruins are quite extensive and lie by the Fakenham road, about 200 yards west of the church. They belong to a private house but can be easily seen from the road.

WALSINGHAM (LITTLE) - LEPER HOUSE

The early history of this House is not known.

It is mentioned in 1486. In 1491 Robert Pigot gave a house for the use of two leprous persons 'of good family.' After this it is frequently mentioned in old wills.

In 1539 Thomas Sydney was governor of the hospital at Walsingham. It was later turned into a Bridewell. The site is in Bridewell Street, formerly Stonegate. On entering Bridewell Street from the Guildhall end, the last house on the right occupies the site of the leper hospital.

WALSOKEN, NEAR WISBECH
Hospital or College and Chapel

Dedicated to the Holy Trinity.

This fraternity seemed to have been important, as several Popes appear to have taken this Hospital or College under their protection.

There is hardly any documentary evidence about this order and the date of foundation and founder is unknown.

Certain indulgences were granted to all its benefactors. The

Bishop of Ely, in 1487, granted 40 days indulgence to all who contributed towards the support of this fraternity.

Just before the Dissolution it had messuages and property in six parishes amounting to 125 acres.

The fraternity consisted of a Master, chaplains and several brethren and sisters.

At the Dissolution it was valued at £5.6.8d. In 1552 it was granted to Mary, Duchess of Richmond and Somerset.

There are no remains above the foundations. The site was on the east side of the Norwich road, opposite Colville Road.

WENDLING ABBEY, NEAR EAST DEREHAM

Premonstratensian Canons

This Abbey was dedicated to the Honour of the Blessed Virgin Mary.

It was founded about 1267 by Sir William de Wendling. He gave them 10 acres of land for the precinct and endowed the canons with the church of St Clement in Conisford, Norwich, and also several other lands and messuages and services in other places.

The Abbey then received several benefactions, some being from titled people, all of which were confirmed by Edward III in 1332. Six lordships and the patronage and advowsons of eight churches belonged to the endowment.

In 1291 the Abbey was valued at £39.19.7½d.

In 1500 there was in residence an Abbot and six canons.

Pope Clement VII dissolved the Abbey in 1528 and granted it to Cardinal Wolsey towards the endowment of his College at Ipswich. After Wolsey's fall and death, it was granted, in 1546 by Henry VIII, to Christchurch in Oxford.

In 1534 the Abbey possessed the manor of Wendling, 247 acres of arable land, 164 acres of pasture and 32 acres of meadow.

The Abbey was colonised by the canons from Langley Abbey.

All that can now be seen are some heaps of rubble, near Abbey Farm. Some of the foundations were removed at the end of the last century and the materials used for repairing roads in the vicinity.

WESTACRE PRIORY, NARFORD   Augustinian Canons

The Priory was dedicated to the Blessed Virgin Mary and All Saints. There were also two chapels dedicated to St Thomas and St Peter.

It was founded by Ralph de Toney or Toni, a Norman Baron, and Isabel his wife, and their sons Roger and Ralph, some time during the reign of William II (1087-1100). Ralph de Toney was related to William the Conqueror. He was the Conquerer's Standard Bearer during the Battle of Hastings. For services rendered, Ralph de Toney was given 22 lordships in Norfolk alone, with many more in other counties.

It was originally for monks of the Cluniac Order, but changed afterwards for Canons of the Augustinan Order and made subordinate to the Priory of Lewes in Sussex. There is no evidence of Cluniac monks ever living here.

The parish church of All Saints, at Westacre, was appropriated to the priory by the founders. We find mentioned that at one time, 'The sub-prior was devoted to his rabbit warren. He also reared swans on the lake near the priory.'

It was a wealthy priory. In 1291 it was valued at £140.5.7¼d., with possessions and property in 74 parishes in Norfolk. At some time the priory was appropriated with the patronage, or part of the patronage, of 16 churches in Norfolk and 13 manors with lands and rents in 82 parishes.

In 1534 the value was given as £308.19.11¾d. At this time there was a Prior and fifteen canons in residence, all of whom subscribed to the King's supremacy. The Prior and eight canons signed the surrender in 1537 and all were granted pensions.

In 1538 this priory was granted to Mary, Duchess of Rich-

[129]

mond and Somerset, for her lifetime, and in 1553 it went to Sir Thomas Gresham.

This priory was on the same scale as that at Castle Acre. Entrance is from the north, through the still-standing gatehouse. The gatehouse leads into the outer courtyard. Part of the south-west tower of the church still stands. There are parts of walls and fragments which extend both sides of the river Nar.

It is a very interesting site.

WESTON LONGVILLE PRIORY, NEAR GREAT WITCHINGHAM

Alien for Cluniac Monks

This Priory was a cell to the Cluniac monastery of Longaville in Normandy.

Walter Gifford, the second Earl of Buckinghamshire, gave his manors in Witchingham and Weston, with the churches of Witchingham Magna, Witchingham Parva and Weston, with lands tithes and rents in twelve parishes, to the mother house in Normandy which his father had founded before his death in 1102.

During the wars with France it was seized as an alien priory by Edward III (1327-1377).

The priory estates remained in the care of the Crown until 1440, when Henry VI granted them to New College in Oxford.

In 1291 it was valued at £25.10.11¼d.

The exact site is not known. It was supposed to have stood partly in Weston Longville and partly in Great Witchingham.

WEYBOURNE PRIORY, NEAR SHERINGHAM

Augustinian Canons

Dedicated to the Blessed Virgin Mary and All Saints.

Sir Ralph Manwaring, Justice of Chester and Lord of Weybourne, founded this priory and made it subordinate to

Westacre Priory during the reign of King John (1199-1216).

However, in 1314 the brethren established the right to elect their Prior from their own canons, but agreed to pay an annual acknowledgement to the priory of Westacre.

It was endowed with a manor and rectory in Weybourne and the churches of East Beckham and Colkirk, with lands and revenues in about 30 parishes. Two Norwich Bishops were benefactors, Anthony Beck in 1338 and William Bateman in 1354.

The value given in 1291 was £15.10.1½d., with property in about 30 parishes. In 1534 it was given as £24.19.6½d. It was granted to Richard Heydon in 1545.

The priory and the church of All Saints, Weybourne, are closely interwoven in their buildings and cannot be separated. There are considerable remains, mainly of portions of the conventual church and cloisters with domestic buildings attached. The site is very interesting.

WEYBRIDGE PRIORY, ACLE — Augustinian Canons

This Priory was dedicated to St Mary.

It was founded by Roger Bigot fifth Earl of Norfolk, in the time of Edward I.

At the Dissolution it was valued at £7.13.4d. It was granted to the Duke of Norfolk.

The foundations only remain, being a circular structure of flint. These are sited south-west of the new bridge over the Bure on the old road to Yarmouth, and are attached to the Bridge Hotel.

WORMEGAY PRIORY, NEAR KING'S LYNN
Augustinian Canons

Dedicated to the Virgin Mary, the Holy Cross and St John the Evangelist.

This Priory was founded by William, son of Reginald de Warren, in the reign of Richard I (1189-1199).

[131]

To the priory belonged the patronage of five churches and three manors appropriated to it with interests in about 25 parishes.

In 1291 it was valued at £37.8.6d., with interests in 23 Norfolk parishes. However, in 1468 it was annexed to the nearby priory of Pentney on account of its great poverty. This was with the consent of John Nevil, Earl of Northumberland, and his wife, who were the patrons of Wormegay.

In 1416 the Earl of Dorset, Thomas Beaufort, was a benefactor.

At the Dissolution it was valued with Pentney. The site, manors, etc., were then leased to Thomas, Earl of Rutland, by the Crown. In 1550 Edward VI gave them to Thomas Thirlby, Bishop of Norwich.

The site is now partly occupied by a farmhouse and premises. Near the priory site stood the Castle of Wormegay. Here resided the Bardolphs who were patrons and benefactors of the priory. It is a motte-and-bailey castle and was of an unusual size.

WRETHAM WEST, PRIORY, NEAR THETFORD   Alien

Roger de Toney (his grandfather was Standard Bearer for William the Conqueror at the battle of Hastings) gave the advowsons of the church of St Lawrence and the manor of West Wretham, with the mill and all that he possessed in this township, to the Abbey of Conches in Normandy, some time before 1162. It was held as part of the possessions of Wotton Warren in Warwickshire, which was a cell to the Abbey of Conches.

In 1291 it was valued at £9.14.1d., with possessions in three parishes. It was dissolved in 1414 by the Parliament of Leicester during the wars with France, as it was an alien priory.

In 1415 it was granted to Sir Rowland Lenthall for life. In 1443 it passed to the Provost and Fellows of King's College,

Cambridge. Probably a small number of monks lived here at Wretham to look after the priory lands.

There are no remains above the foundations. The church of St Lawrence is in ruins.

WYMONDHAM ABBEY   Benedictine Monks

Dedicated to the Honour of God, the Blessed Virgin Mary and St Alban.

This was first a Priory, founded by William de Albini in 1107. It was for Benedictine monks and at first subordinate to St Alban's, where the founder's brother Richard was Abbot. The establishment had between ten and twenty monks. The Prior of Wymondham Abbey paid to St Alban's a mark of silver annually in token of subjection.

It was richly endowed with churches, lands, tithes, etc., all of which were confirmed by Henry I (1100-1135). About this time it possessed property in at least 45 parishes in Norfolk, with nine manors and the advowsons or part of ten churches in Norfolk.

In 1448 the priory became Wymondham Abbey and thus became independent of St Alban's.

At first the church was for the joint use of the monks and the citizens of Wymondham, the monks entering from their monastery and the populace from the common street. Due to a severe quarrel and strife between the two parties, the Pope (Innocent IV) in 1249, arranged that the town should have the nave, north aisle and north-west tower, and the monks the rest. This did not end the strife.

Towards the end of the 14th century, the monks found that the central tower which belonged to them was unsafe for the bells, so they pulled it down. They transferred the bells to the north-west tower which belonged to the parish. The monks then built the present octagon tower two bays west of the former tower. When they had finished, they blocked off the

[133]

arch with a wall so that the church was divided into two. Thus the parishioners were not allowed to see the high altar.

The monks then re-possessed their bells and re-hung them in the new tower, but walled off the north-west tower to prevent the townspeople from using it for bells of their own.

Of course, the result of this was a series of riots against the monks. Finally the town was given official sanction to have their own bells. So the townspeople, still angry, rebuilt their west tower and built it higher and greater than that of the monks. It was never completely finished, although it stands 142 feet high. Before this tower was finished, the monks and townspeople came to an agreement.

There were many noble benefactors to this monastery. Eighteen obits were observed in the Abbey church annually. There were also the chapels of Our Lady, St Margaret and St Andrew.

Around the time of the foundation there was a Prior and twelve monks. In 1291 the value was given at £153.1.2¼d., with possessions in 43 Norfolk parishes alone.

The value in 1534 is given at £211.16.6¼d. At this time the Abbot and ten monks subscribed to the King's supremacy. It was granted in 1543, to Thomas Howard, Earl of Surrey. In 1564 Queen Elizabeth granted it to Sir Walter Haddon.

The Abbey, or what remains, is left in a perfect setting. It is dominated by its two tall towers of the church, one at the west end, the other at the crossing. Of the other buildings, little more than foundations exist. It is a very interesting site and well worth visiting.

In 1549 William Kett, after the Rebellion, was brought to the great west tower of Wymondham from Norwich Castle in irons. He was drawn up by a rope fixed about his neck, to a gibbet which was erected on the top of the tower. There he hung until his body wasted away. His brother Robert had the same treatment performed at Norwich Castle. William Kett was a butcher by trade and lived in Wymondham.

[134]

WYMONDHAM HOSPITAL CHAPEL AND CELL

Dedicated to God and St Mary.

The Hospital was for lepers and impotent people of the Order of St Lazarus of Jerusalem. The fraternity consisted of a custos or master and two or three brethren. They supported themselves mainly by begging from travellers.

It was founded by William de Albini in 1146, with the consent of William Turbus, Bishop of Norwich. The founder gave to the church of St Lazarus of Jerusalem at Burton Lazars, in Leicestershire, about 120 acres of land a mile north of Wymondham.

A cell was erected by the founder near a bridge over a stream near the Hingham road at a place called Westwade in the manor of Choseley. The custos of the cell was considered to be the lord of the manor of Choseley.

The brethren were directed to pray for the souls of King Stephen and Queen Maud and of Queen Adeloza, wife of the founder.

In 1534 it was valued with Wymondham Abbey. The property was granted in 1544 to Sir John Dudley. He sold it a year later to William Kett who was hanged at Wymondham Abbey in 1549. Thus his lands went to the Crown. Queen Elizabeth later gave the manor to the Hospital of St Giles in Bishopsgate in Norwich.

The foundations can still be traced in a meadow.

GREAT YARMOUTH

Medieval Yarmouth had nothing to do with the sea. Its face was turned to the river, with the town itself being between the river Yare and the sea.

The walls stretched in an arc from the river back to the river, shutting the houses off from the sea.

These walls were begun after 1260 and completed in the 14th century. The whole circuit was only 2,280 yards long and about 23 feet high and had sixteen towers and ten gates.

[135]

Stretches of this wall are still preserved with the usual gaps from the west-east stretch north of Mariner's Road, then running north along Blackfriars Road and St Peter's Place to south of the Hospital School, the Market Place, turning west again to Town Wall Road. The final north-west tower is at the north end of Rampart Road. Within these walls the townspeople of Yarmouth lived their lives with the religious houses of the Benedictine monks, Dominicans, Carmelites and Franciscan friars, with a medieval hospital and two leper houses.

YARMOUTH (GREAT) - WHITE FRIARS PRIORY
Carmelite Friars

Dedicated to St Mary.

This Priory is thought to have been founded in 1278 by Edward I (1272-1307). In 1337 the Carmelites enlarged the house and in 1509 it burnt down.

The priory had several benefactors including a number of nobility.

In the priory church were buried Dame Maud, wife of Sir Lawrence Huntingdon, in 1330, and Sir John de Montucute and Ralph Nottingham.

The monastery was sited in the north part of the town near the North Gate.

YARMOUTH (GREAT) - HOSPITAL OF ST MARY

Dedicated to the Blessed Virgin Mary.

This Hospital was founded by Thomas Fastolff early in the reign of Edward I (1272-1307).

William Gerbrigge, Burgess of Yarmouth in 1278, in his will gave an annual rent for the maintenance of two priests in its hospital. After that it was often mentioned in wills, especially in 1349 during the great plague. Eighteen houses had been given to it by 1392.

John, the Bishop of Ely, granted an indulgence of 40 days

[136]

to anyone who could assist in the support of this hospital in 1419.

The hospital consisted of a warden, two or more priests, eight brethren and eight sisters.

At the Dissolution it was valued at £4.13.0d. After the Dissolution the hospital buildings and chapel were turned into a school.

The buildings are in the trust of the Corporation of Yarmouth.

YARMOUTH (GREAT) - LEPER HOUSE

Two Leper Houses existed at or near the north gate of the wall. They are both referred to in old wills. The exact site is not known. There is no documentary evidence about these leper houses as to their foundations or their exact site.

YARMOUTH (GREAT) - PRIORY   Benedictine Monks

The Priory was dedicated to St Nicholas the patron saint of fishermen.

It appears that originally there was a small chapel here which is thought to have been dedicated to St Benet, in which was placed a chaplain to pray for the souls of persons frequenting this coast. It seems as if it was neglected after this.

In 1101 Bishop Herbert de Losinga founded the church and priory of St Nicholas, as a cell to Norwich Cathedral Priory of the Holy Trinity, and the services were performed by a deacon and three chaplains appropriated by the prior.

The monastery consisted of a prior and three or four monks, later increased to eight, with three parish chaplains and one deacon. There were many benefactors to this church. The actual dedication service did not take place until 1251.

St Nicholas' is the largest parish church of England, covering an area of about 23,000 square feet. In monastic days there were seventeen chapels in the church and many lights burning before images, with at least sixteen Guilds. Most styles

[137]

of architecture are seen in the church, but unfortunately it was gutted by fire in 1942 during the second world war. It was rebuilt in 1957-1960, under the directions of Mr Stephen Dykes Bower.

At the Dissolution it was valued with Norwich Priory. In 1538 it was granted to the Dean and Chapter of Norwich, who, in turn in 1551, leased the priory and parsonage to Robert Lowel for 80 years.

The church itself is well worth a visit. To the south-east of the church can be seen the refectory. There is only a fragment of the orginal left, having been completely renovated and modern windows inserted. Other than this there is nothing left of the original monastery. The refectory is part of Priory School, Priory Road.

YARMOUTH (GREAT) - BLACK FRIARS PRIORY
Dominican Friars

Dedicated to St Dominic.

The House of Blackfriars is thought to have been founded in 1270 by Thomas Fastolff and Geoffrey de Pykering. The priory church was completed in 1380 but in 1525 it was burnt down.

There were several benefactors, including burgesses and bailiffs of the town.

In 1542 it was granted to Richard Andrews and Leonard Chamberlyn. It was sited at the south end of the town at Blackfriars Road, near the city wall.

YARMOUTH (GREAT) - GREY FRIARS PRIORY
Franciscan Friars

Dedicated to St Francis.

There is some doubt as to the founder of this Priory. It is thought that Sir William Gerbrigge did found it, *c.* 1226, although it is not mentioned with its house until 1271. Sir William was Bailiff of Yarmouth.

[138]

In 1256 the Bishop of Norwich, Walter de Suffield, was a benefactor.

According to Stow, Edward II (1307-1327) was the founder.

In 1541 it was granted to Thomas Cromwell. Shortly after Sir Richard Williams was granted the whole site and precinct with all the buildings. They later passed to the Corporation of Yarmouth.

The site is down the opening by the side of No 12 South Quay, near the river. The remains are very scanty, being part of the cloisters and some bits of wall. The church was to the north, across Queen Street. It was 177 feet long but there are no remains.